I'M HERE TODAY:
Finding Hope In My Battle With Cancer

Patricia Santistevan

I'm Here Today
by Patricia Santistevan

ISBN 978-1-58169-363-8
For Worldwide Distribution
Printed in the U.S.A.

Axiom Press
P.O. Box 191540 • Mobile, AL 36619
800-367-8203

This book is dedicated to all those cancer survivors out there and to all those who have gone before me.
I also dedicate this book to Dr. Pardue, Dr. Greenfield, Dr. Lopez, and Dr. Muller, who put out their best efforts to help me fight this battle against cancer.

Here are the names of my friends and relatives who have died of cancer since I myself was diagnosed:

Carol Linn	February 2004
Mother of Brian and Lisa Halpin	2004
Iola Sabiers	September 26, 2006
Pat Powell	October 7, 2006
Wanda Lucero	December 29, 2006
Gerald Ortega	December 31, 2006
Ginger Good Iron	May 8, 2007
Christine Trujillo	June 20, 2007
Gloria Martinez	July 16, 2008
Trina Garcia	October 5, 2008
Elizabeth Ann Perraglio	January 5, 2009
Susie Garcia	April 19, 2009
Katherine Bryce	May 2, 2009
Genevieve Sandoval	May 14, 2009
Nancy Martinez	February 24, 2010
Darolyn Thomas	May 31, 2010
Rosemarie Scott	June 10, 2010

Acknowledgments

My thanks go to:

Rebecca Gallegos, Mary Romero,
and Abraham Santistevan for typing;
Kathleen Watson, Joshua Santistevan,
Larry Socea, and Richard Teschner
for editing.

Contents

Introduction

There are few things in life that can shake you to your foundation like hearing a doctor say that you have a terminal illness. After three years of terrible suffering, from an illness that continually evaded the best efforts of doctors who tried but failed to properly diagnose it, that is exactly the news I received. On December 23, 2003, I heard the fateful words from Dr. Pardue in his Santa Fe, New Mexico, office: "You have ovarian cancer and need surgery as soon as possible." Ovarian cancer is called the silent killer because it is so difficult to diagnose.

My symptoms had begun gradually. But over time, they repeatedly subsided and returned, continually worsening until my stomach became so enlarged that I thought I had a weight problem. I barely ate because of the pain and feeling of fullness, and my son Joshua would get upset with me because I wasn't eating. Finally, as difficult as it was to accept, I almost welcomed the news that my terrible bloating, cramping, and constipation had a name and a prescribed course of treatment.

Six days after receiving the diagnosis, I underwent an operation for removal of the tumor. While the doctor was operating, his assistant saw how extensive the cancer was, and suggested that the doctor should just "close me up." But Dr. Pardue said, "No. We have to give her a fighting chance." A day after surgery, social workers offered no encouragement, telling me that I would need twenty-four-hour care the rest of my life, and that I only had one or two years left to live.

So, where do you turn for hope when there is no hope? I turned to the God of heaven, the God of hope. I immediately started calling everyone I knew to ask them to pray for me. My friends and co-workers, in turn, called their church prayer ministries and requested prayer for me.

Several months later, Dr. Pardue informed me that my situation had improved: I actually had a 5 percent chance of becoming totally cancer free, and one to seven years left to live. I took that 5 percent chance and made up my mind that it would be 95 percent. By May 2004, Dr. Pardue was amazed I had healed so well. A CAT scan confirmed that the tumor was totally gone. With that news, I felt my future was now different; it was hopeful. I had faced death and been given a new life. It reminded me of the new spiritual life we can have in Christ when we recognize the cancer of sin in our lives and go to the Great Physician for His healing. Through the trials of a relapse and the uncertainty of the future, my faith in God and the support of my friends and family, as well as all of their prayers, continue to encourage me through this difficult and fearful time.

Now, after more than five years of struggle, two major surgeries to remove tumors, and moving into my fourth round of chemotherapy, I find the lessons I have learned throughout this journey to be even more applicable than ever. The God who asks us to suffer is familiar with pain and suffering and does not require it of us lightly. He knows what He is asking and has good purpose. There are things we learn in suffering that cannot be learned any other way. To those struggling with cancer, I offer this encouragement: Rely on your faith to get you through the difficult days. Take one day at a time and enjoy the things you like most, whether it is shopping at the mall, taking nature walks, eating yogurt ice-cream cones, or reading good books. Finally, surround yourself with family, friends, and prayer, and remember this: While you have breath, you have hope. This is my story of hope.

Chapter 1

Roots

Family has always been an important part of my life. I was raised in the high mountains of Des Montes (which means "mountains" in Spanish), New Mexico. It is a little town twelve miles north of Taos. I am the second oldest of two brothers and five sisters. My older sister and I lived with my great-grandmother Francisquita, whom we called "Quita," in an old adobe house with a dirt floor until she passed away in 1966. (Adobe is mud and straw mixed together and formed into blocks. The blocks are stacked and covered with this mixture inside and out.)

We were isolated from the rest of the world. We had no running water, and my father used to go down to the river to haul the water up in barrels. During winter, thick ice would form on top and we had to use a hammer to break the ice to get to the water. We'd bring the water inside, and my mother would warm it up during bathtime. Since we didn't have a bathroom inside the house, my mom would turn the lights off in the kitchen, put a round tub in the middle, and place chairs around the tub. She'd drape a blanket over the chairs for privacy, and everyone would go into the living room to watch TV while we took turns bathing.

In the winter we made popsicles out of the icicles that hung from our roof by dipping them in unsweetened Kool-Aid. We also made snow cones by pouring the Kool-Aid over snowballs. In summer we took the dry sap off of the pine trees and added sugar and made our own chewing gum. Since we didn't go into town much, we made do with whatever we had.

The house we lived in was L-shaped, and consisted of two adjacent houses with a connecting wall. My parents and younger brothers and sisters lived in the two-room house, and my great-grandmother lived in the other four-room house. One room was actually used for food storage with a very small cellar that stored pinto beans and potatoes. The icebox was small with a block of ice on the bottom that had to be replaced weekly. A small wooden box was used to store butter and cheese outside in the winter, the box was tied to a rope, which was pulled in through an open window for easy access. After my great-grandmother passed away, my dad opened a door between the connecting houses, filled in the cellar with dirt, and made the food storage room into a bathroom. He then floored, re-roofed, and stuccoed the house.

Building a Family

Tom and I were married in 1980 when I was twenty-two years old. Before and during my first pregnancy, I dreamt that I had a baby boy. My husband and I prayed asking God if this baby was to be a boy, and we felt God's confirmation. In those years, in Taos we didn't have ultrasounds so there was no medical way of knowing our baby's gender before birth. We told all our family and friends that we were having a boy and decided to name him Joshua, meaning: "The Lord is my salvation." I was twenty-three when our first son was born. Although we had told practically the entire town that we were having a boy, everyone still kept asking what we had, even after the baby was born. They were astounded to find out that we, indeed, had a boy. God's promises are true.

Again God showed us we were to have another boy, whom we named Abraham, meaning: "Father of many nations." During my third pregnancy, my husband's stepfather was diagnosed with throat cancer and given one to two years left to live. It was sad watching my father-in-law go through radiation therapy and failing health. Again God showed us we were to have a son. In

1983 our third son was born, whom we named Uriah, meaning: "The Lord is my light." He, indeed, was a light to us in a time of darkness. My father-in-law passed away a few months after Uriah's birth.

In 1985 we moved to Albuquerque so Tom could attend college. He went to school and worked part-time. It was difficult financially, so I ran a daycare business in my home for two years to make ends meet. The daycare business allowed me to stay home with my babies, bake cookies, and teach my sons from preschool workbooks.

I finally ended my daycare business because I needed to get out of the house more, and it was becoming too stressful. I went into business as a Mary Kay consultant. I held skin care classes and made deliveries after my husband came home from work so he could watch the kids. I also did facials in my home when I put the kids down for their naps. I explained to my sons, who were then only a few years old, that Mommy needed to work to have money for food and clothes. It's amazing how well little kids understand when things are explained to them. My sons were very good and stayed in their room while I worked. Of course, on occasion they would peek out from their room and see all these women, faces all powdered in white with their Mary Kay masks on. They'd giggle and go back to their room. I suppose they got a big kick out of it. I continued selling Mary Kay for many years.

Finally, in 1989, when my youngest son started kindergarten, I went to work part-time as a salesperson. My neighbor and close friend watched my sons after school until I arrived home from work. Sometimes we exchanged babysitting.

In 1987 my husband, Tom, joined the Army Reserve to get extra money on the side and to get the student loan repayment program to help pay for college. He was transferred to El Paso in 1990, where he worked in the active military as a recruiter. I also transferred with my sales job to El Paso. After seven years in sales—three in Albuquerque and four in El Paso—I resigned from that position and went to work part-time as a bank teller, which eventually turned into full-time work.

My First Tragedy

It was during this time in El Paso that my younger brother, Joe, was killed in an automobile accident. I was filled with grief and disbelief. By the time we made it back to Taos for the funeral, Joe's casket was closed and I didn't get to see him. Weeks went by before I could cry, and it took me a full year to accept his death. I frequently dreamed that he was still alive. The previous Christmas we had taken a family photo. Years later we took a similar family photo and, strangely enough, where my brother would have stood there were balloons in his place (see pictures on page 98). It was at this time that I found release by writing the following about my brother, whom I loved dearly.

Our Last Christmas: 3-18-1996

There you stood, tall and slender, as you cupped your hand across your mouth and gently brushed it against your mustache. With that smile I knew so well. That gentle smile...and your eyes that seemed to understand every word I spoke. You listened well, you understood, everyone's hurt and pain. What was it, the last thing I heard you say: "People are more important than anything, make time to be there, to listen to them."

And here we were, our last Christmas together as brother and sister. As we mingled, I watched you, and somehow I knew: This would be our last Christmas together. How I knew, I don't know. There was a special calling from God above. I guess it was you He was calling.

So we took pictures, brothers and sisters, the entire family. One last time, one last smile, one last look. One last touch of your hand upon my shoulder, as we stood side by side. Cameras were flashing, "Smile, Joe," I said. Those were probably the last words I ever spoke to you…

The next time I saw you, I…didn't see you, you were already gone. Just your picture next to your casket. Disbelief, I couldn't cry, so unreal. I felt so numb, sitting there; I didn't even get to say good-bye. It was then, I realized…it wasn't good-bye, it was only: "See you later."

Wait for me, Joe. Someday I'll meet with you in the clouds and together we'll fly across the sky to our everlasting home. I love you.

Dedicated to my brother Joe.

CHAPTER 2

Compromised Immune System

We relocated to Santa Fe in October 1996, when my sons were teenagers. My husband continued working as an Army Reserve recruiter. My job search landed me a job as a full-time teller at a credit union downtown for two years. A few months after I transferred to a branch closer to home, problems began, caused by what may have been my chemical sensitivity. While other tellers complained of frequent headaches, I frequently became fatigued, dizzy, and nauseated by mid-afternoon. I saw the doctor and tests were performed, but everything came back normal. I was told I was perfectly healthy. Since I was sleeping only six hours most nights, I thought I was just exhausted and needed more rest.

One day while working I became very fatigued and dizzy. I held onto the counter's edge to steady myself as I stood there helping a constant stream of customers. I desperately looked around, hoping someone would relieve me so I could take a break, but everyone seemed too busy to notice. I held on as long as I could. Finally a lady walked in, and I let go of the counter to type her account number into the computer. I heard myself say, "Oh no!" as everything became blurry and I felt myself sinking to the floor. As I fainted, I didn't remember hitting the floor. I awoke flat on the floor with outstretched arms. I felt embarrassed as I tried to get up and couldn't move. I managed to slowly move my arms in closer to my body. I tried moving my head but felt too weak.

I heard my name shouted several times as co-workers took notice of me on the floor. The manager knelt by me and placed cold wet paper towels on my forehead and kept me talking. I could barely talk but felt the compassion and concern as we awaited the ambulance. The paramedics tried to get me to stand, but I was too weak. I felt my body being lifted onto the gurney as I was transported to the ER. I was kept in the ER for several hours on oxygen. Again, tests revealed no obvious cause for my symptoms.

After this, I experienced several more episodes. I was driven home by co-workers or picked up at work by family. I ended up in the ER a few more times, where I was given oxygen and sent home again. The last time I was in the ER I was told that I had a small amount of carbon monoxide in my system, but the doctors refused to document it in my file, saying it was not a significant enough amount to document. But, I was also told that if I had any more carbon monoxide in my system I'd be in a coma. Again more tests were performed, but nothing else was found.

The credit union where I worked had a drive-thru that was not sealed off, and fumes from vehicles entered the building. By mid-afternoon there was enough of an accumulation that it was making me sick. I didn't realize what was making me sick until I smelled the fumes from a large truck that was at the drive-thru for an extended time. It was then that I felt the same symptoms as I had during previous episodes. The doctors told me that I needed to leave the area affecting me, so I transferred to another branch. By that time I was so sick that my nose burned, and I was constantly dizzy. Even fumes from vehicles in the parking lot were making me sick. Soon after my transfer, the symptoms started to clear up and eventually disappeared. As I look back I believe that this extended, repeated exposure to carbon monoxide compromised my immune system.

Eventually, I resigned from the credit union and, after a couple of other jobs I held for a short time, I went to work at the forest service as a full-time personal assistant. Shortly thereafter, I began experiencing constipation, gas, stomach bloating, and cramping.

The symptoms were mild at first and the cramping seemed to be from certain foods I ate. Also every other month during my menstrual cycle, I became very weak and the cramping was so severe that I missed a day of work to recuperate. My periods became much heavier than usual. When I explained this to my doctor, she said it was normal even though I told her it was not normal for me. I later found out that a Pap smear does not detect ovarian cancer. The symptoms were so severe that I stopped eating out and developed a fear of food, worried that whatever I ate would intensify the pain. When I went out for lunch, I'd walk into a restaurant and the smell of food repelled me so much that I'd walk right out, go back home, and have a small snack instead. Strangely enough I didn't recognize that what I was actually feeling was nausea. Maybe I was in denial.

It wasn't until years later that I found out the forest service building where I worked had a mold problem. It had been subject to water leaks for a number of years, and the problem was not addressed properly. The leaks worsened, and it wasn't until after my diagnosis that action was taken to correct the problem. However, after several years, the building continued to have problems. I learned that a water leak from the upstairs break room had leaked downstairs directly in front of my workstation. The tiles in the ceiling were eventually replaced. I now understand why it was that after I returned to work I continued to get sick in that area. I felt that my immune system was so affected that I became dizzy, weak, and nauseated while in the building. I took my work home and entered the building only when absolutely necessary. As time went on, I'd get sick after only an hour in the building.

The Road to Diagnosis

How discouraging and frustrating it is to know that your body is signaling that something is wrong, but finding no test or treatment that either identifies or relieves the problem. Eighteen months before my initial diagnosis, I saw my primary care doctor for an annual checkup. During that examination, I discussed the bloating and cramping I had been experiencing for some time. My doctor prescribed a regimen to treat my symptoms without determining their cause. I followed that regimen and felt better for a while, but the symptoms eventually returned.

Next, I had periodontal surgery, and the symptoms disappeared for a few months. So, because gum bacteria can enter the stomach and create problems, I thought perhaps my stomach problems were attributed to the periodontal disease. Later, when I saw the dentist for cleaning, he said I had a cavity. When it became infected, the dentist prescribed antibiotics and I was given a root canal. The tooth pain was severe. I finally recovered, but then my stomach problems returned and worsened. I continually skipped dinner and finally managed only a morning snack and a light lunch. The pills I was taking became ineffective.

That year when Thanksgiving arrived, I did none of my usual baking. I didn't even eat, for eating brought on such unbearable discomfort that I always broke down and cried. By then my stomach was so distended, I looked three months pregnant and felt like I was nine months pregnant, yet my Pap smear was normal. My primary care doctor ordered a colonoscopy and referred me to Dr. Pardue.

Despite my physical condition, after Thanksgiving my job required me to travel to Phoenix for training. While in Phoenix, I was so bloated and my stomach cramped so badly that I was totally skipping meals. When I talked about my sufferings with friends there, they immediately realized that something was seriously wrong, and they urged me to see a doctor as soon as I returned home.

The next week in Santa Fe, after my colonoscopy results came back "normal," Dr. Pardue ordered a CA 125 blood test (a test that shows a patient's level of cancer cells—normal CA 125 counts for healthy individuals are below 32). But for someone already diagnosed, it must be below 21. My CA 125 reflected cancer levels approaching 1,248! An ultrasound clearly showed that I had ovarian cancer and also identified a significant amount of excess abdominal fluid. About six cups of abdominal fluid were extracted, relieving the pressure within and easing my breathing. Now we had to deal with the cancer that was causing all the problems.

Dr. Pardue rearranged his schedule so surgery could be done immediately following Christmas. Rather than fearing surgery, I actually looked forward to it for relief. Here it was Christmas Eve, and I didn't know how I would tell my family the news. When my husband, Tom, and I told our sons about my cancer, they reacted quietly, in wide-eyed shock. But I avoided further talk of it, not wanting to ruin everyone's Christmas.

In actuality, the suddenness of the diagnosis and surgery gave us little time to prepare mentally or emotionally. While I took the time to find my life insurance papers and clean the house, the truth was that I actually cared little about the house's state of cleanliness. I had a major cancer battle ahead and focused all my thoughts and prayers on this. While the average age of women suffering from ovarian cancer is over sixty, I was only forty-five at the time.

Chapter 3

Surgery and Uncertainty

On the day of surgery, Tom held my hand while we waited until 6 p.m. for Dr. Pardue to finish his other scheduled surgeries. Dr. Pardue asked me if I was ready for surgery, but I was more concerned whether he was ready, since he had been in surgery all day. When he finally operated on me, he discovered massive disease everywhere—from the first fatty layer, the omentum, to all female organs; to even being attached to the diaphragm, large intestine, one kidney, and my liver. There was also a massive tumor attached to my bladder. Dr. Pardue performed a total hysterectomy and even scraped the walls of my abdomen but was unable to remove all of the cancer.

Six hours later I awoke with Tom beside me. Strangely, my parents seemed distant, their voices garbled. Later I thought I heard my sister Teresa weeping and the family comforting one another. I thought they had come to say their good-byes. Needing reassurance, I asked my father to say something, anything. He seemed unsure, but finally said, "Patsy, I'm here; I'm here." Although this was comforting, I kept asking Tom, "Am I going to make it?" I was thinking that I only had days left to live because of the immense pain I was feeling.

The next day, while Tom stepped out for a moment, two social workers came in. I was so weak and in so much pain that their faces were blurry, even though they were only inches from mine. However, I could see their concern. I asked many questions about the cancer. Their answers were heart-wrenching. It was like a nightmare as their faces fluctuated before me. All I could think of was how were my sons going to get along without me? It was horrifying to think of dying so soon, yet I wasn't afraid to die.

"Will I be able to go back to work?" I asked.

They responded, "No, you'll need someone to take care of you for the rest of your life because the cancer is in the liver."

This statement made such an overwhelming impression on me that for three months I continued to believe that the cancer was in my liver, even though it was actually on the outside of the liver. They also told me that I only had one to two years left to live, which upset me greatly. I could barely comprehend what I was being told. When Tom returned to the room and found me crying, he was furious at their insensitivity in discussing something so traumatic without family members present, let alone sowing the seeds of inaccurate information in a mind made fragile by pain and physical trauma.

At first, discouraged by my prospects for recovery, I refused chemotherapy. I felt that if there wasn't any hope, why should I put my body through more torture? But Dr. Pardue was like the kind, old-fashioned country doctor, and he patiently reminded me that there was hope. He convinced me that I would live through all this. Dr. Lopez, an oncologist, came to see me in the hospital. He gave me hope that I had a good chance of making it if I took the chemo. However, while I don't remember ever seeing him, I do remember the encouraging words I heard. My husband told me this later. Dr. Greenfield, another oncologist, also encouraged me to take the chemo. Despite how bad the cancer was, the doctors restored my hope and told me I had a fighting chance of up to seven years.

I felt that I was too young to die and that there was still so much work here on earth to do. I thought that Satan wanted to take my life because God had a plan for me, and the devil didn't want that plan fulfilled. However, the love, prayers, and encouragement that I received gave me the strength I needed to keep going to fight this cancer, no matter what happened. Faith, hope, and love got me through this and will keep me going until God's plan for me is fulfilled and He calls me home.

The very first chemo treatment was given while I was still in the hospital. Almost immediately my blood count dropped, and I needed two blood transfusions.

Tom was immensely comforting at this time, caressing my hands and face and telling me that I would make it, I would live. His compassion, love, and great faith lightened my load. Our sons anticipated my every need from lip salve to water, and they relieved Tom for quick trips to the bathroom or to shower and shave or to release his stress by jogging. Tom and my sons kept vigil at my side, constantly enveloping me with their great love.

The unbearable pain continued for many days without my being able to turn from side to side for relief. Even though they connected an IV with a PCA (Patient Control Anesthesia) that I could use to release morphine, any time I used it, it stung so fiercely that I had to hold my breath to tolerate the stinging. Everything else about my initial recovery was a blur. I was so overwhelmed with pain that I was unaware of what day it was or who visited me. Tom later told me that so many people tried to visit, they had to limit my visitors to family members to allow me to get much needed rest.

Although the pain gradually decreased, the IVs on my arms became infiltrated (clogged) and my arms got so swollen that the nurse had to take the blood pressure from my leg. She moved the IVs from the backs of my hands to my wrists and then to the insides of my arms. Finally, the doctor removed the IVs entirely and surgically implanted a PICC line (Peripherally Inserted Central Catheter) on the inside of my arm to administer chemotherapy. The IV lines are easily connected and disconnected to the PICC line. The PICC line had to be wrapped with Saran Wrap when I showered, and it needed to be flushed daily.

Slowly, however, I somehow began walking with the family's help: first from the bed to the door, then a few steps down the hall, and finally circling the nurses' station. Initially I was connected to an IV on each arm, a catheter, and oxygen. As I walked, I needed to push or pull the IV and oxygen cart. These movements caused such entanglements that often only the nurses could separate them. But, looking outside at the sky, clouds, rocks, and trees, was like seeing the world for the very first time—everything seemed so incredibly beautiful to me that I felt an overwhelming sensation of still being alive, of being given a second chance.

Soon I was walking all hours of the day and night to relieve the numbness and swelling in my legs. Tom and I strolled around the hospital halls holding hands for the first time since surgery. My oxygen and IVs went everywhere with me, making me feel like one of the BORGs (an android/cyborg, from Star Trek). A second hospital gown covered my backside, and it seemed cape-like. So, for me, it became the cape of Super Girl, Superman's cousin, causing a transformation in me: I became empowered to fight this cancer. I desperately desired to live long enough to see my three sons get married and looked forward to holding grandchildren, teaching them, and playing with them.

It was at about this time that, coincidentally, my sons brought me a stuffed dog. We named him Krypto, like Superman's dog, to guard over me. Krypto strengthened me with hope, a constant reminder at my bedside. I also received more stuffed animals, as well as numerous get-well cards and notes. Even though there was not enough room for all the flowers that were delivered, they poured in anyway.

This time of recovery in the hospital came with many challenges. Once, when removing the oxygen to wash my face, I forgot to replace it, and then became breathless and dizzy. Another time I bent over and accidentally pulled the IV out of my arm. Tom saw the blood gushing out of my vein and realized what had happened.

So it was with great rejoicing by a cheering squad of nurses when the catheter was removed and I finally voided, and also when the oxygen was removed.

Embarking on the Road to Recovery

Finally, after ten unbelievable days, and ten pounds lighter, I was discharged from the hospital. But it wasn't until I improved that everyone's shock wore off and their feelings surfaced about my cancer. (Refer to the Appendices for Tom's and our sons' stories.)

Simply wearing clothes again returned my identity. My shoes, however, wouldn't go on because my feet were so swollen. But the cold, crisp air brushing past me felt wonderful, and riding only a mile to our home gave me a sense of well-being—of being alive. Coming home was comforting. It felt as if I had been away for months. It was wonderful to see Pepper, our dog, and the sunroom filled with my plants. Although the laundry had piled up tremendously in ten days, simply thinking of doing it restored a sense of normalcy for me.

As I settled down near a crackling fire to watch TV with the family, my head and arms suddenly began itching and an overpowering nausea followed, both reactions to the chemo. The nausea came from the smells of everything from food to perfume, even to my own urine.

Peaceful sleep escaped me those first nights home. Monsters chased me, as I desperately locked doors and windows in nightmares, interrupted by an equally desperate need to use the restroom. Even Tom, lying next to me, wasn't comforting, as the slightest bumps in the bed set off waves of pain.

Finally, I discovered that yogurt would relax me for sleeping. But with nights tamed, the days worsened with pain. It eventually reached unbearable levels as I discovered yellow drainage dripping down my legs. A home nurse arrived, pressed most of the fluid from the incision, and had the doctor prescribe antibiotics. There was very little that helped reduce the surgery site pain, which lasted nine weeks. So Dr. Pardue prescribed codeine for pain, while I tried soothing the incision area with microwaved dry rice packs. This extended period of pain felt like a terrible setback, yet I was grateful to still be alive. When I was in extreme pain, I often cried out loud for the Lord to help me bear it.

Besides the surgical pain, I experienced itching near the PICC line, which turned into a rash and became painfully infected. So the PICC line was removed and I had to take antibiotics again to fight the infection. In the hospital a Port-A-Cath was implanted on my right clavicle collarbone to accommodate the chemo. A Port-A-Cath is an implantable venous access system intended to permit repeated access to the veins for the parenteral delivery of medications, fluids, and nutritional solutions, and for the sampling of venous blood. However, I became allergic even to its sutures and endured yet another round of antibiotics. I worried about how chemo would be administered if even the port failed.

One of the most striking side effects of chemotherapy is hair loss. When my hair began falling off in huge clumps, I felt identity loss. In utter despair I cried. But Tom just seated me at the edge of our bathtub and began clipping off my shoulder-length hair. Then he shaved my head clean. Once past that, I soon found that having no hair complemented no energy. It was far easier. Wigs became a novelty for going out, while I wore turbans at home. My teddy bears wore my wigs while I wore the turbans, and I thought: More wigs definitely require more teddy bears! During the first shower I took following the shaving, out of habit I automatically dumped conditioner on my bald head. A seemingly endless rinsing barely removed all the slipperiness from the conditioner.

The second chemo came quickly, followed by major exhaustion. My strength returned, but it was coming from prayers said by people all over the world. I actually felt those prayers physically. Members of our church and my work family continuously prayed for us. They also committed to providing meals for our family that began while I was still in the hospital and continued for months after I returned home. But one of the things I really missed was my winter's baking of pies, muffins, cookies, and even breads. Finally a friend baked my favorite oatmeal cookies when a movie we planned to see was sold out. Again the Lord answered the smallest of prayers.

Often, during painful nights, I would write in my journal. A friend blessed me with the journal as a gift and, at first, I used it as a memory aid of who visited or called, or who brought flowers or gifts. I recorded all the positive things done and said by others, even the occasion when prayers for my health were included on the church prayer chain. While the Cancer Institute encourages journaling for healing, I realized my journal was slowly becoming a book. For years, since taking a creative writing class in high school, I had dreamed of writing a book, and it seemed to be evolving by itself.

Throughout all this Tom was very supportive, taking me to appointments, opening doors for me, or simply helping me walk on bad days. While I was often so ill that I could barely think, Tom would always remember to ask all the critical questions of the doctors (and even some of the non-critical ones). And, while family and friends cleaned our home for us and ran our errands, loneliness and boredom overtook me. So my son Uriah and Tom took me shopping, pushing and loading the shopping cart to get me out of the house and doing something normal.

Then the friends I had made on the job visited with such a huge box of leisurewear that I was unable to hold it because of my weakness. I was so happy to see everyone. Valentine's Day came and a co-worker returned with a picture of a live tree adorned with valentine hearts and a huge wicker basket filled with the paper hearts in white, pink, red, and purple—one from each of the sixty-one employees. The back of the picture read, "This tree was dedicated to you. Happy Valentine's Day." Money was raised for my increasing medical bills. I read all of the hearts immediately and then as the days and months passed, when I felt blue, I'd reach into the basket and pull up a heart and read it again. It was a constant reminder and encouragement of all the people who loved me and were praying for me. Later, they again raised money with a Frito pie and bake sale to help with all the medical bills, which surprised and honored me. Endless cards and gifts brightened the days and made nights more bearable, with everything becoming more hopeful.

Major exhaustion and pain, which accompanied the third and fourth chemo treatments, interrupted the progress of my recovery. The only way I could control the pain was to sit quietly and pray and by listening to soft worship music while lying in bed. Nevertheless, after the fourth chemo, I thought that I was strong enough to attend church with the family. But during the service, a terrible dizziness overcame me, and Tom had to hold me up and take me home early. As soon as we arrived home, I went straight to bed. This was so disappointing that a great sadness overwhelmed me and I began crying, so Tom and our sons placed their arms around me and prayed to comfort me. Apparently the hysterectomy had brought on early menopause, prompting symptoms like the unexpected crying. Other symptoms included my head and shoulders often feeling like they were on fire. Sometimes the only comfort I felt came with talking to understanding family members by phone. Many times I found myself dialing constantly until I could reach someone.

The crying and moodiness worsened until it developed into major depression, accompanied by feelings of helplessness and hopelessness. Dr. Pardue wanted to prescribe antidepressants and counseling. But I felt that the ten medicines I was taking were already too many. It seemed that every time I went to the doctor, I went home with a new prescription for something else. So I relied instead on the overwhelming strength of everyone's prayers and, finally, my peace and thankfulness returned.

By the time the effects of a previous chemo treatment had worn off and I began feeling really good again, it was time for another treatment. I missed having a normal life and I missed having my hair. However, things slowly began returning to normal as my energy increased, and I started driving again after three months. It was very liberating to be able to do things for myself again. So many people were praying for my family and me, and I truly felt the power of those prayers as my body became stronger.

One day, just before the fifth chemo, I became sad thinking of not being outdoors and running errands again. After the chemo treatment my body ached and my throat hurt. Food didn't taste the same, and I had a bad metallic taste in my mouth. My stomach was upset, and I just didn't feel well at all. During this trying time, my husband held and comforted me and I felt better. I continued drinking a lot of water. That weekend it rained and was bitterly cold so Tom made a fire in the fireplace. The crackling of the fire was comforting and made the day seem not so dreary.

Chapter 4

Hope Comes in the Spring

Then came that first spring after my surgery. Spring is my favorite season, with its smells of blossoms and the greening of plants and trees luring me outdoors. Tom and I strolled around our huge yard and browsed over the tulips, irises, and budding trees. During that walk, when I ducked under a branch, my wig hung up on it. I desperately looked around to see if any neighbors were outside and saw my bald head, but thankfully they were all inside.

Hearing the chirping birds at their bath in our yard, I recalled one of my favorite scriptures: "Look at the birds of the air; they do not sow, reap or store away in barns, and yet our heavenly Father feeds them. Are you not much more valuable than they?" (Matthew 6:26).

Spring truly became the season of my rebirth. I began planning to garden again and prayed for the strength I would need to nurture tender plantings.

There are two scriptures that I read daily to sustain me. The first is:

> *He that dwelleth in the secret place of the most high shall abide under the shadow of the Almighty. I will say of the Lord, He is my refuge and my fortress: my God; in Him will I trust* (Psalms 91:1-2 KJV).

God indeed was my refuge and fortress. During this very difficult time, I turned to God for strength and courage to get me through another day. When I had extreme pain, I cried out to God to give me the strength to bear it. The other scripture is:

> *For I know the plans I have for you, declares the Lord, plans to prosper you and not to harm you, plans to give you hope and a future* (Jeremiah 29:11).

I would read that scripture two to three times a day, and every day I would question the Lord,

> How, God? How do You plan to prosper me? Where does my hope and my future lie? Am I going to make it through this? The doctor said I only had a five percent chance of being cancer free. He is only giving me one to seven years of survival. What is my future going to be like? Yet I have hope in You, Lord, hope and faith that You will get me through. Faith that You will do a complete healing in my body, hope and faith for complete restoration. I have faith for the finances needed to pay all the medical bills. I have faith, Lord, that You will set me free from worry and fear. For with God all things are possible and nothing is impossible with God.

God blessed me so much with those scriptures.

Along with the flowers of spring came New Mexico's high winds and some humor. Because I had now lost my eyebrows and eyelashes along with my hair, I decided to buy false eyelashes. A very kind beautician applied my eyelashes and makeup. I was so excited and went grocery shopping with my new look. Thereafter, instead of mascara, I carried eyelash glue in my purse. However, I found that my false eyelashes fluttered so much in the breeze that I feared they would fly off like two little butterflies. At times they blew backward into my eyes, and I soon learned that extra-long lashes weren't compatible with high winds. Once, my husband interrupted me while I was putting on an eyelash, and I almost glued my eye shut! I even fantasized awakening from naps and finding my eyelashes stuck to the pillow.

During my next checkup I was so exhilarated to learn that the CA125 count was only 5, far below normal. Dr. Pardue told me that the cancer could be considered gone and was amazed at my healing. He said, "Go enjoy life and grow your hair back." I gave him a big smile and spent the entire rest of the day spreading this good news by phone. When Tom and our sons returned home that evening, they were elated. Tom was so happy that he started laughing and picked me up and swung me around.

In spite of such great progress, a bout of dizziness forced me to leave early from a family Easter egg hunt in the beautiful Des Montes Mountains. I was so disappointed and left so tearfully that soon everyone else was crying. But when Tom and I arrived home, we saw our sons' Lego's and a pizza box on the table, and we knew that, at least, they had their own good time. The next day, however, my strength returned, and we all saw the movie *The Passion of the Christ.* I felt that Christ addressed me directly when He said, "See, I make all things new." I knew then that both my strength and hair would return. On the way out of the theater, I found eleven dollars on the floor. There was no one else around, and my oldest son was walking ahead of us so I thought he had dropped it. When I asked him he remarked, "Nope, that's not mine; it's yours now, Mom!" So the Lord even blessed me with eleven dollars that day.

Despite the new low CA levels, Dr. Greenfield, my oncologist, extended my chemotherapy to eight treatments because of the cancer's massive extent. I cried out of great disappointment, but my sister comforted me by taking me shopping. Later, I felt renewed thankfulness, knowing that chemo was nearly over and that I had an enjoyable summer ahead to look forward to. Although my recent weight gain would make it harder to fit into summer clothes, Tom and the doctor saw it as a positive sign of restored health.

I celebrated my first birthday after surgery with delivered bouquets, a cake, even more flowers from my son Joshua, and endless calls of congratulations. I was just relieved to have made it that far, but the most beautiful part of my birthday was feeling loved and appreciated as never before. The next day I lunched with my dear old friend Lisa and her husband, Gilbert, an Elvis impersonator. Lisa and I look alike, but I was still surprised when her friend stopped to greet us and asked if I were her sister. I was surprised because although I was wearing a wig, people still thought I resembled Lisa. Well, that's another story I'll tell some other time.

Prior to my next chemo treatment, I shopped, cleaned, did laundry, and watered my plants. God gave me the strength to get through each day. The sixth chemo brought with it weakness, wobbliness, and nausea, but after only four days I developed a ravenous craving for burgers and fries. When my taste buds returned to normal after a treatment, everything tasted so good. And when my energy returned, I went out and ran errands. I was so relieved to feel better and went for short walks. My tired, aching body welcomed the fresh air and sunshine. That sudden change felt to me like Job 42:10,12:

> *The Lord made Job prosperous again, and gave him twice as much as he had before.... The Lord blessed the latter part of Job's life more than the first.*
>
> *Weeping may remain for a night, but rejoicing comes in the morning* (Psalm 30:5).
>
> *And we know that in all things God works for the good of those who love him, who have been called according to his purpose* (Romans 8:28).

We are more than conquerors in Christ Jesus. Anyone who thinks that the Scriptures are not relevant for today should think about just a few of the passages I have quoted and consider how aptly they apply to a situation like mine.

The seventh chemo brought on terrible anxiety and an inability to sit still. The nurse attributed it to an accumulation of steroids used to strengthen my body throughout chemo. Afterward, I felt enveloped by sadness without reason, and I missed my sons terribly even though they were only away for the day. Again, Tom stood by supportively while everyone continued their prayers for me.

The eighth and final chemo was in June. Although the dose was lower, it still caused weakness and wobbliness. Nevertheless, I told the nurse I would run from the chemo room, so happy that chemo was over. Afterward I anxiously inspected my head every day for the first signs of hair growth. I could hardly wait for my hair to grow back, but I wondered if I would have so much hair that I'd look like a hairy beast! I continued seeing the doctor every three months for regular checkups. Then my cancer levels fell even further—to only 3! A CAT scan confirmed my cancer remission. I truly felt like a walking miracle.

Tom took me for one- to two-mile walks almost every day. I felt my stomach and leg muscles firming up. My energy increased and I felt stronger. The fresh air and sunshine felt wonderful. June also brought our twenty-fourth wedding anniversary. For months I prayed for no illness on that day. As the day progressed, so did my feeling of well-being, and I finally put on a favorite dress, a new red wig, flashy jewelry, long eyelashes, and five-inch platform heels. When Tom returned from work I met him at the driveway, the first time I had dressed up in six months. With his eyes tearing, he kept kissing me and saying over and over how beautiful I looked. While we dined out, the church again blessed our sons with dinner delivered, so I didn't have to worry about dinner for them when they came home from work. A few days later, as I got out of the shower, I looked at my eyebrows and went "Ahhh!" My body's very last hair fell from an eyebrow. The poor thing had been hanging on for dear life!

Chapter 5

Return to Some Level of Normalcy

Finally, with chemo's end, I returned to work half-time, a day I had long anticipated. Besides the joy of seeing good friends again, I felt a sense of normalcy and well-being. But on the third day, I became so weak and dizzy that I had to be driven home. When I attempted to return to work several times, the same symptoms came back. I finally realized that this was the same chemical sensitivity problem that had developed before I was diagnosed with cancer.

Remember that I had previously worked at a credit union with a drive-up teller window connected to the building, and during peak hours, auto exhaust fumes leaked inside. While it didn't bother others, I had been taken three times to the ER for dizziness, fainting, and breathing problems. The last physician I saw contradicted himself by saying the carbon monoxide levels in my blood were too negligible to be included in the report, but if they were any higher, I'd have been in a coma. I changed jobs several times after that and finally settled at the Forest Service as a human resources assistant. I loved the job, my boss, and all my friends there.

But with the return of weakness and dizziness, the only solution seemed to be working at home part-time. (I much later learned that a roof leak directly above my workstation at the Forest Service caused a mildew growth on ceiling panels. When the air system circulated, it blew mold spores directly upon me. How much these immune system–weakening agents attributed to the start of my cancer is unknown.) I was blessed with the most compassionate supervisor ever. He worked with me through this dilemma, even allowing pay for my listening to instructional tapes while lying in bed taking notes. Despite working at home, however, I barely managed to handle those twenty hours along with housework, grocery shopping, and laundry. It was overwhelming, but only a matter of readjusting. I could hardly wait for my immune system to return to normal and for the anemia to clear up.

In August my CA levels remained at 3, but my liver levels were elevated. Although the doctor feared that the cancer had migrated to my liver, a CAT scan was normal. Apparently my liver was overprocessing medications, so they removed the port and stopped blood thinners and all the medications. Within days my energy dramatically improved, and my liver began functioning normally.

Pepper and My New Miracle Dog

Pepper was part-poodle, weighed ten pounds, and was black and white. On September 22, I lost my dog of thirteen years to heart disease. She had lost weight, was suffering, and had difficulty breathing. I laid my hands on her, told her I loved her, and prayed that God would end her suffering. She looked up at me, got up, and walked over to her pet taxi, and collapsed at its entrance. I knew this was it and felt it was time to just let her go in peace. She fell into a deep slumber and her breathing slowed. I kept glancing at her while watching television as her breathing became slower and more peaceful. I patted her skeletal body and felt her last breath as I told her I loved her again.

Within the hour after I prayed for her, she passed away. Her body was still warm, but within seconds became cold as I sat there petting her. I told my son Uriah that she was gone. We both sat on the floor a long time, petting her and weeping. Then Uriah took a pillowcase from the nearby chair and placed it over her body. I was glad she no longer suffered and she died while sleeping peacefully, but I missed her terribly.

We buried her in the backyard. The next few days, I felt so lonely and sad without my little baby girl. "Precious" is what I had called her. Out of habit, I kept looking for her in the house, but she was gone and I had to let her go. I washed all her blankets, dog dishes, and pet taxi, and threw away her medication. Then I stashed everything in her pet taxi uncertainly for another pet. I no longer had my little dog to keep me company when I was home alone. So I turned to God to fill the empty space in my heart.

After Pepper died, I went through a grieving process. I no longer felt safe when I was home alone with the door open. She had always barked to inform me of anyone outside. Now I kept looking at the back door, which was locked. I kept looking for my little dog to let her outside, but she was gone. I'd pass by her pet taxi and tears would come. I couldn't concentrate on work and felt sad. I didn't think I'd ever want another dog, but after a few days, I felt so lonely I went to the animal shelter. With my situation I wanted a small indoor dog. I kept returning to the shelter daily but couldn't find a little dog.

Finally, I woke up feeling happy one day and heard a still, small voice telling me that that was the day. I was getting ready to leave home for the animal shelter when the phone rang. It was my co-worker, Monica. She had a little dog her sister had brought for her to give me. In five minutes I was at the office staring at my miracle dog. The answer to my prayers was right there looking at me. He was nine months old, half Chihuahua and half Shih Tzu, white, with a broad muscular chest. My son Joshua suddenly noticed how he resembled Krypto, the stuffed dog I was given at the hospital. So we named him Krypto, just like Superman's dog. I made a red Super Dog cape for him with the S emblem like Superman's. So now Krypto keeps me company and makes me feel safe again!

Public Ministry and Testimony

In September, I had the opportunity to hear Joni Eareckson Tada, a quadriplegic, speak at the Albuquerque Convention Center. She had broken her neck in a diving accident and subsequently wrote a book about her accident. A movie was eventually made about her accident and her resulting faith. She even has a radio series. Her life's accomplishments despite her severe limitations are truly amazing, and I had followed all this since I was a teenager. I was living in Roswell with my husband and first son when I heard an announcement over the radio that she was getting married and her friends would be her hands to open all the presents. Her voice had been full of excitement and anticipation over the air, but hearing her share her story live so eloquently in Albuquerque gave me such renewed hope and reassurance.

Upon entering the large auditorium I bought her book, *The God I Love.* When Joni was wheeled onstage with her husband, Ken, I realized what a great gift God had given her—one who both loved and cared for her, yet was so much a part of her ministry. While in line for an autograph, I could hardly contain my excitement! When I was second in line, Joni was speaking to a woman on my left. Ken stood to my right, and I introduced myself to him. Then Joni turned and looked directly at me and asked if I was blessed. I answered with, "Oh, yes!" She signed her book by Ken placing a pen between her teeth. I also gave her a copy of the book I was writing—my own great struggle with cancer. Back home, Tom said I glowed with excitement.

A week later Tom and I attended the Glorieta Cancer Retreat in Glorieta, New Mexico. This free retreat for cancer patients and their families is held twice a year. It was interesting talking and praying with other cancer patients. Although I felt weak during the conference, it was wonderful to see the beautiful countryside and attend informative classes.

The following week Sophie, a friend from church, accompanied me to KCHF, "God Answers Prayer," where I gave my cancer testimony live on TV. One of the spiritual gifts God has given me is that of encouraging others. I was nervous but prayed that God would speak though me and that my story would bless the listeners.

Chapter 6

It's Spring Again

It was spring 2005. I had survived another winter. I bought birdseed, but this time I placed the ten-pound bag in the shopping cart myself and pushed it outdoors. I filled the feeder and birdbath and stood at the kitchen window, doing dishes and singing praises. I watched the birds happily chirping and drinking. I thought, *Oh, to be a bird, so free and not a worry in the world.* The tulips had already blossomed, and I awaited the blooming of the trees and remaining flowers. I again planted seeds and, with the rainy season coming, anticipated a lot of flowers. But it was so cold and windy during this time that I only took Krypto for his walk once a week.

I had gained twenty pounds since surgery, so I was desperately trying to lose weight to fit into my summer clothes. I became much healthier and stronger each day, no longer needing naps. I was amazed at my new energy. I could also face the winds full-force, not worrying about my wig getting caught in a tree or my eyelashes fluttering away because I finally had my own head of hair. My first haircut after the chemo was on November 4, 2004. My hair was curlier than it had been before I became ill, and it was a darker salt and pepper. My husband told me that angels styled my hair. I was also glad that my eyebrows and eyelashes had come back stronger and healthier than ever. But my fingernails were still weak and brittle.

Overall I looked and felt healthy—I just tired easily and needed to remember to rest. I became excited with all the things I could do, but, hey, I had spring cleaning to catch up on from last year! I continued to work part-time at home using a laptop computer to work at my own pace. I thanked God that I still had my job along with the freedom to enjoy a slower paced life. That was my new "normal." My whole life had changed because of cancer, but I became a better person because of it. With God's help I was confident that I'd get my story out to those who needed to hear it.

A Setback

It's amazing what a difference one year can make in a person's life. It's as if my memory was temporarily erased and returned. For almost a full year, my entire mind and body had been consumed by coping with the pain and trying to regain my life and strength.

As I looked back, so many things had changed, mainly myself. I was amazed that I had even made it through surgery. Now, as I got back into baking again, I thought of the time when everything seemed to stand still. My baking flour had expired during my illness and recovery, and I had to throw it out. As I cleaned my cupboards, I found things I forgot I had. I threw out old medicine, vitamins, and expired food.

I had double-duty with spring cleaning this year. I had done no spring cleaning the previous year, and this year I discovered a whole new way of cleaning. No longer could I clean the way I used to; now it was at a much slower pace. I actually enjoyed it as I discovered things I had forgotten I had. And, as I got organized, I felt calmer with a deep sense of peace, knowing that my family would appreciate all of my hard work.

However, at this time I began to display all the symptoms of fibromyalgia. My doctor said that it was probably due to the fact that I'd had chemotherapy and was still going through a three-year healing process. I increased my vitamin intake and exercise activity (walking more often) to counteract the symptoms. I also watched my diet carefully.

In August 2005 I returned for another CA 125 screening. My

previous count had been a 6 in May. Unfortunately this time it was 32, with normal for me being below 21. My doctor was concerned and asked if I ever smoked or had pneumonia. I said no, but that I became breathless, tired, weak, and dizzy sometimes. He wondered if it was hyperventilation syndrome caused by stress and anxiety. He scheduled additional bloodwork and a CAT scan. As I sat wondering what would be next, I felt a little fear but much peace, knowing that people were already praying for me. I couldn't help but wonder if I would make it this time. All I knew was that I was in God's hands. Whatever the outcome, God was with me. He promised in Scripture that He would "never leave nor forsake me." But I definitely did not want to face more chemotherapy and becoming sick again. I had been feeling so healthy and energetic except for the breathlessness. I'd come a long way and seemed to be doing pretty good considering all I'd gone through.

I had been walking at least three times a week for forty-five to sixty minutes and felt better afterward. Dr. Greenfield told me that I was overweight and out of shape, but I knew it was more than that. I didn't experience the breathlessness while walking, but only when picking up heavy objects or going to the office, where I couldn't breathe very well because of lack of air circulation and the heat. Sometimes I did too many things at once and experienced symptoms. It made me wonder what was going on.

My next doctor visit revealed the CA 125 count at 48. Dr. Greenfield gave me a hug and asked if I was afraid. "Yes, a little," I said. He explained that the CAT scan results revealed a lemon-sized mass in my pelvic area and that there was also thickening around my heart's sac. So he scheduled an echocardiogram, which Dr. Pardue later told me was normal and that I actually had a very strong heart. However, after a physical examination he could feel the tumor in my pelvic area but farther in, close to my colon. Dr. Pardue scheduled surgery for October 3. I also saw Dr. Greenfield, who explained the option of chemo after surgery. He said that they would inject the excised tumor with different types of chemo to determine which would bring the best results. Surgery frightened me because of what I had gone through before. I just didn't understand this. "Why, God?" I prayed constantly for healing. But no matter what happened, I knew that I was in God's tender loving hands.

Second Glorieta Cancer Retreat

In September I attended my second cancer retreat, this time with my mother and sister Marcella. We had a wonderful time and took lots of pictures. It sure helped to get away and take my mind off the pending surgery. I was given a journal, *My Healing Companion,* in which I jotted down phrases and thoughts of my feelings at the time.

When I returned home, however, I felt depressed. I cried and cried until I was emotionally exhausted. Then I lay down and fell asleep. When I woke up, I called the 1-800 Cancer Hope Hotline and spoke with a lady who had similar ovarian cancer with reoccurrence and two surgeries. It helped tremendously to speak with someone who knew what I was feeling.

I took Krypto for a walk and during the walk realized how much stress I was feeling. Things had happened so fast, and I couldn't believe what was happening to me. I began to wonder how much time I had left. I wanted so much to be happy and enjoy the good days I had. I thought about my family and how they'd get along without me. It would be difficult, but I'd try my best to make it easy for them. I'd clean house, do the shopping, pay bills, make lists, and water the plants—so much work to do, yet I'd try my best to communicate without making it seem like I was in my last days. It would make it easier for me as well, knowing I did the best I could for them. It wasn't easy trying to think of everything in such a short time, but plan I must and plan I did. After surgery I expected to be so overwhelmed with pain that I wouldn't be able to think straight, much less be able to remember where everything was, so I made myself little reminder notes. My hope was that all this effort would help make life easier for us after the surgery, regardless of the outcome. I prayed that God's grace would carry us through this very difficult time and that His great mercy would rest upon us.

I also asked my doctor for one more CA 125 in hopes the numbers would go down so I wouldn't have to go through additional surgery. On September 27 the CA 125 count was 67.7, so I felt God could still do a miracle through surgery as I prepared myself for yet another round of it.

Chapter 7

A Continuing Miracle

On October 3, I arrived at the hospital for surgery and was immensely pleased to learn that the attending nurse was a friend from church, Christina. She prayed for me and encouraged me. Both my mother and I had teary eyes when they took me to surgery. I had to use every ounce of strength to keep from crying. My husband, parents, and friend Sophie prayed while I underwent surgery. The next thing I remembered was awakening from surgery. Dr. Pardue said that it all went well, and he didn't have to resection my colon. Also, the tumor had shrunk to the size of an olive, and its outside was soft where it had begun to dissolve. (I believe that this was due to all the prayers and the supplements I took.) The tumor had been attached to my colon, but it was easily peeled off, making only a small perforation, which was easily repaired.

The best news was that the cancer was self-contained and had not spread. The lab tests showed no cancer remaining. It did show, however, I was highly resistant to Taxol, the first chemo drug used. So Dr. Greenfield discussed using the drug Doxil. Dr. Pardue suggested waiting a few weeks for the incision to heal before beginning chemotherapy. I, however, refused any more chemo because of the damage it had done to my body, but I also had faith that God could restore my health.

I was in the hospital five days with this surgery and lost five pounds. My first roommate had had a partial hysterectomy and kept saying that she had strong recuperative powers. All night long she asked if it was time for breakfast yet. The next day she argued with her husband, talking loudly and banging doors. I couldn't sleep and was exhausted. So they moved me to another room. My husband, Tom, was not allowed to stay the night because there was another patient in the same room with me. By about the fourth hospital day, my second roommate went home and I was alone. But, as I slept, I kept waking to whispers. I could feel a tap on my left shoulder. I'd wake and look around, only to find myself alone in the dark with the door shut. After several times of tapping and whispering all around my room, I realized what was happening. I could feel peace and the intense presence of the Lord. I knew that the whispers were all the people praying for me and the tapping was from angels' wings watching over me. I just smiled and went back to sleep. Two weeks prior to surgery, I had begun having problems with a dislocated left shoulder from an injury many years prior. I believed that the tapping on my left shoulder meant that the Lord was healing my problem.

After I returned home, one night as I slept I felt my breathing becoming very shallow and slowing down. I felt my spirit leaving my body and going toward a bright light. I smiled and happily yielded. Within moments my spirit returned to my body, and I awoke with a start and began breathing normally again. This continued several times throughout the night. I felt that the Lord was telling me that it wasn't my time yet. I still had work to do here on earth.

Complications

Two days after I got out of the hospital, on a Sunday around 5:30 p.m., I awoke from a nap with stomach pain and a foul odor. As I stood up, I noticed my clothing was wet from a brown liquid draining from the incision. I changed my clothes and with help from my sons, I placed thick gauze over the incision and they rushed me to the ER. When I arrived, they brought a wheelchair for me since I was unable to walk due to the pain. They kept me overnight and pumped me full of antibiotics to fight the infection. They also removed all twenty-two staples from my incision and inserted a wick to drain the fluids from the infection. I returned home so weak that my mother stayed with us for a week to help me. A visiting nurse came weekly until the end of November to check the progress on my healing from the infection, and my husband changed the wick daily.

In October my CA 125 count was down to 34, and by November it had returned to normal at 12. Nevertheless, I fell sick with yet another infection after a piece of the wick stayed stuck inside the incision. When I tried to pull it out, it broke off. My nurse also tried removing it but couldn't. Eventually, Dr. Pardue was able to extract it, and he prescribed a new antibiotic for the infection. However, I had an allergic reaction to the new medicine and broke out in a rash. My throat hurt, my eyelids swelled, and my left eye was half-shut. I lay in bed for an hour with a cold washcloth on my eye until I could open both eyes enough to get up. The healing came very slowly because I was taken off antibiotics completely. Finally, one morning after much prayer, a wick piece popped out of the incision, and it began to heal!

We spent Thanksgiving and Christmas with family in Taos that year since I didn't have the energy to cook. By Christmas Day, I had another full-blown infection that made my stomach red and swollen and very painful. My doctor finally put me on antibiotics again. In spite of all this trouble, my CA 125 count went down to 6—great news!

It's a New Year, 2006

Finally, after three long painful months, my incision healed, or so I thought. By that time I had joined a cancer support group, which helped tremendously. I desperately needed the support group as the emotions of my diagnosis became more of a reality. Confused and apprehensive about what to expect, I gained a better understanding of my own prognosis as well as the shared burden and pain we all carried. Knowing that I was not alone made it easier to bear. At first I offered support and encouragement to others, but as time went on and I entered chemotherapy for the second time, I sought support and encouragement, which my group kindly offered. I also attended weekly Bible studies. I got out whenever I could to have lunch with my sister or friends.

It was then I discovered my environmental sensitivities increased as I became weak, dizzy, and short of breath. When I went to the mall where there were a lot of perfumes in the air, I was unable to enter certain stores; and after about one to two hours, I needed to leave the mall for some much-needed fresh air. I carefully planned afternoon trips to stores when I felt my best. I took water and snacks along to help my energy levels wherever I went. I also noticed that fumes from our wood-burning fireplace made me sick.

In February my CA 125 count rose to 11, still within the normal range. I was prescribed more antibiotics after I noticed blood and pus in the incision, which wasn't healing. Finally Dr. Pardue decided to core out the incision through minor surgery. That procedure exposed foreign material remaining from the wick, which clearly indicated why the incision wouldn't heal.

The next day, Saturday, I awoke with yet another full-blown infection and severe pain. My abdomen was swollen, irritated, and burgundy colored. My husband took me to the ER, where they pumped me full of antibiotics again and sent me home with a prescription for more. On Sunday morning I got up to take a shower and barely made it out of the shower. I became so dizzy and weak that I had to call Tom for assistance. He put a dry towel on the pillow so I could lie back down with my wet head and slept the rest of the morning. I got up and ate a nice breakfast that Tom had prepared and slept again in the afternoon. I thought if I lay resting quietly the incision wouldn't open again. But upon arising from a nap, I noticed the incision was open and seeping fluid. I finally decided it was going to do what it wanted to, so I stayed up and moved about the rest of the day. By 9 p.m. I was so exhausted that I had to go to bed.

On Monday, Dr. Pardue opened the wound so it could drain. The rest of the week I saw him daily. I thought, *Here I am with an open wound again.* I cleaned it twice daily and kept it covered with gauze. This time it really started to heal. Nevertheless, I was tearful and tired of the constant pain. But Dr. Pardue told me something that was both encouraging and spirit lifting. He said that I might not believe him and I might even laugh at him, but that he was going to tell me this anyway. He said, "I know you believe in a Higher Power, and so do I. Everything happens for a reason. The fact that you had so many infections could be a good thing because they made your immune system kick in to fight those infections. When your immune system kicks in, it also fights off cancer cells." I told him that I agreed 100 percent. I was so grateful for a doctor with the faith to believe. Miracles do happen! This gave me renewed strength and left me feeling so good that I went home and washed the kitchen floor!

My incision finally healed by May eighth. When I returned to Dr. Pardue, I blew up a balloon and wrote the words "I AM HEALED" on it. When he walked in, I gave him the balloon. When he checked my stomach, he was surprised to see yellow smiley-faced stickers around the incision site. He smiled and said that he loved my sense of humor.

When I saw Dr. Greenfield again, he asked me about chemo once more. He said that since I'd delayed having chemo for so long, a renewed course of chemo might not kill the remaining cancer cells the second time around. Nevertheless, I still felt it was wise to refuse chemo, considering all the damage it had done.

In May, my sister Teresa and I volunteered to work at the Glorieta Cancer Retreat. Although my incision had just healed, I was determined to give my time in return for all God had done for me. I wanted to be of service to others, so my sister and I helped in the exhibit room and at the registration desk. I was pretty tired when the weekend was over, but it was well worth it. I thanked God that He had given me the energy and strength to do it.

A Respite and a Relapse

In April my CA 125 reading went up to 12 but my CAT scan revealed that everything was normal.

In June of 2006 we realized a dream come true—a cruise to the Bahamas, through another answer to prayer. The cruise was a Christmas gift that Tom had given me before my cancer diagnosis. Each year of my battle with cancer, Tom had paid to extend the departure date. With Tom being on active duty in the army, the potential existed that the military might either station my husband in California or move his unit to Iraq. With such uncertainty came a sense of urgency to quickly make our dreams a reality. Our future again was in God's hands.

So, on June 2, our family flew to Florida to visit Sea World. We then boarded a Carnival cruise ship, "The Sensation," and set sail for the Bahamas. We began the cruise with an ID photo that probably didn't register all the awe and excitement on our faces. Our long-awaited cruise had finally become a reality. The only other vacations we'd taken during twenty-five years of marriage involved military duty for my husband or simply out-of-town visits to family. I sensed that if we didn't go this year, we might lose the vacation package altogether.

The highlight of our trip for Tom and me was the celebration of our wedding anniversary. We all dressed up for dinner, and Tom presented me with a bouquet of fresh roses and a ring. We ordered a cake that said "Happy Anniversary." The waiters treated us very special at dinner that evening, and they and my husband sang "My Girl" to me. The highlight of the cruise for our sons was the

Captain's Dinner. And we all enjoyed the last night on the ship at a big party with dancing and singing and a huge midnight buffet!

After we came home from our cruise, my CA 125 reading showed that the cancer count had risen to 23. In July, I moved to California with my husband for a month and returned to Santa Fe using Angel Flight for more doctors' appointments. The initial intent was to move permanently, not partially, but I had to be in Santa Fe for appointments and eventually more chemo. Angel Flight is free air transportation on privately owned two- to four-seater airplanes whose owners fly cancer patients and their family to cancer-related doctor's appointments.

On August 8, 2006, my CA 125 reading went up to 40, again above normal. In anticipation of the test results, I awoke that morning from a dream of going up a steep hill to the top of a church. I entered the church and asked where the bathroom was. The door was locked, but someone opened it with a huge key. They said the door would remain unlocked as long as I was there. When I went into the bathroom, I saw that it was full of medical instruments and looked like a hospital or surgical unit. I thought, *I need to hurry and get ready for the wedding—do my makeup, fix my hair, and get dressed.* This room was behind a big auditorium. I went out of the bathroom and peeked through curtains into the church and saw that it was almost full, yet people were still pouring in. The music had started and the worship began. I went back into the bathroom thinking, *It's almost time. I need to hurry.* I came out and found that the only way out was through a window. There was an extremely steep incline going down. I looked at my watch, seeing that I had only ten to fifteen minutes left before the wedding. Just then I heard voices and footsteps coming toward me. They were on their way with the wedding gown. When I awoke I felt that it was Jesus coming to take me home.

CHAPTER 8

A New Beginning

My life was full of new beginnings and adventures, even with cancer. I did not know what the future held for me, but I knew it was in God's hands and that I needed to take it one day at a time. When Tom was first told that the army was transferring him to California, I asked the Lord: "Why California? Why so far from family and friends? What about my health? How will we manage financially if we keep our Santa Fe home yet rent in California?" I realized that I had to prepare for all this, so I did so through prayer. After several weeks of prayer, I realized that I needed to trust the Lord even more than before. Again, the Scripture comforted me:

> *And we know that in all things God works for the good of those who love him,[a] who[b] have been called according to his purpose* (Romans 8:28).

I was confused about where to begin, so I listed everything we needed to do for the move. Finally, getting the essentials down, I started making piles in the family room so that when the packers and movers arrived, everything would be ready. Then, we gathered our sons and prayed together for a safe trip. This would be the first time our family had been separated in this way, and we had mixed emotions. Leaving our sons and dog behind was not easy, but we knew they would take good care of each other and the house while we were gone.

When we arrived in San Francisco, my body ached from the

long drive, so we walked to Fisherman's Wharf. Then we set out to find Travis Air Force Base and locate an apartment. It was the Fourth of July, so the Web was our only option for finding an apartment. After much prayer we accepted the only available apartment we found and moved in the following day. Little did we know what a blessing that place would be and what friendships we would form there. We felt like newlyweds unpacking, except this time we were much older. We had many new things just like we had had when we were first married, and we felt that sense of adventure all over again. Tom was given an entire week off from work, so we explored our new community.

We visited my ninety-two-year-old aunt, who was also my godmother, in Oakdale, California. I found out she was a breast cancer survivor. I had not seen her since I was in elementary school so we had much catching up to do. Afterward we crossed the Golden Gate Bridge, headed for Chinatown, where we walked all over and bought souvenirs. For dinner, we went back to Fisherman's Wharf and had clam chowder in bread bowls. A few days later, we found trails along the Bay Area where we went for long walks.

Across the street from the apartment, we discovered a grocery store that sold live seafood from tanks. It was fun watching customers place live crabs in take-home bags. I imagined the crabs escaping in the trunk. (I suppose you have to count how many go into the bag and how many go into the pot.) Can you imagine if one of those crabs got out of the bag and was hiding somewhere in the trunk of your car! But the surprise came at home when Tom tried to place the crab in the boiling pot. It grabbed hold of the utensil and had to be knocked off. Then it desperately held onto the pot's edge and had to be knocked loose again. I had forgotten to tell him to pour boiling water over the crab before the struggle began. I thought: *What if it jumped out of the pot and hid under the furniture?*

When Tom reported for work the next week, I unpacked and arranged the apartment. It was quietly peaceful and relaxing. I discovered that there were many blind people living in our apartment complex while attending school for the impaired. All day long they walked by with their canes, feeling their way to and from the laundry. One day, when I was at the laundry, a blind man bumped his leg into my bucket that was next to the dryer so I moved the bucket to the top of the dryer. But he recoiled and bumped his hand into it once more. He struggled to find what was in his way, so I apologized and explained what I had done. It was an uncomfortable situation and showed me that I had much to learn. I began observing and even speaking to blind passersby. Some said hello back, while others just kept going.

Then I met Brittney, a nineteen-year-old who had been blind since birth. When we met, I immediately wanted to take her under my wing and be her friend. The next day we went into the swimming pool together. I described the pool surroundings as we descended into the water, her arm on mine. From that day on we became close friends. She later showed me her apartment, with her talking computer. Of course I had to turn the lights on, as it was totally dark. She confided that her favorite cookies were oatmeal chocolate chip. So I baked some and gave her freezer bags of them because I knew that soon she was leaving for home to Southern California, and I was returning to New Mexico. I also filled sandwich bags with the cookies for the Angel Flight pilots who would be flying me back to Santa Fe for my next doctor's appointment.

CHAPTER 9

Angel Flights

After a month in California, I said good-bye to Tom and began my three-segment Angel Flight. The second flight had turbulence, which painfully jerked the seatbelt into my stomach. I could barely walk after deplaning because of the pain. I also needed a restroom badly, since such small planes lacked restrooms. That first week home I could barely walk because of bloating and abdominal pain.

Within days my two oldest sons moved back home to help me. Then at a Sunday zoo outing, I noticed painful swelling under my left breast. Thinking my bra's underwire had caused it, I changed the type of bra I wore for several days. But the pain was unchanged. Dr. Greenfield ordered a CAT scan, which revealed spots on the outside of my spleen. My CA 125 again rose, this time to 69. Once more I had a port implant and began new chemo rounds with Carboplatinum and Gemzar. These drugs weren't as strong as the ones used in the initial rounds of chemo that I had undergone, but I was still apprehensive about possible side effects. Nevertheless, I now felt that I had no choice but chemo if I was to beat this cancer. I was told that this time around my hair would thin instead of falling out. But fortunately my hair didn't thin at all.

The treatment plan called for three successive weeks of chemo with one week off for recovery. But with my blood cell counts continually falling due to the first treatments, the doctor shortened the regimen to only two successive weeks of chemo before a recovery week. After each treatment, I had three days of either white or red blood cell injections. In spite of these setbacks, after only three chemotherapy treatments, my CA 125 count fell to 5.

Prior to beginning the chemo treatments, my church family again prayed for me. Amazingly the spleen pain disappeared even before chemo began. After each treatment, my church family again blessed us by providing meals so I would not have to cook when feeling so sick.

One day after a blood cell injection in my arm, I took the Band-Aid off and saw that the stain of blood had formed into a perfect heart. I smiled to myself and felt that it was God's way of showing how much He loved me.... This was the second time in the last few months that the bloodstain had formed into a heart; the first time it was on a Band-Aid from a cut finger (see picture on page 101).

By October, I felt well enough for an Albuquerque Balloon Fiesta outing. I was very tired afterward and needed to rest at my sister's house to regain energy before the drive back to Santa Fe.

On October 30, I showed up at the Cancer Institute for my appointment in high spirits, dressed in my Roman Halloween costume. Everyone was amused and impressed. I don't normally dress up for Halloween, but since it was the day before Halloween, I decided that it would be fun and different for me. It was the only costume I owned and I had worn it to my sister's fall celebration right before my cancer diagnosis in 2003. Afterward I went to a "Look Good, Feel Better" class in the evening.

In November, I attended a Creative Recovery Workshop at the Cancer Institute, where we made kites and flew them out in the parking lot. I told the instructor that from that moment on, every time I went to the Cancer Institute I'd look at the sky and remember the day I flew a kite.

I tried to keep as busy as possible since I no longer worked out of my home. Due to the cancer, my disability retirement was approved on July 8, 2006. I wanted to enjoy life as much as possible and did as much as my health allowed. I began attending cancer support groups soon after my second surgery. Over time the support group became like a close-knit family. I was the only one in the group who had been diagnosed with ovarian cancer. Most of the women suffered from breast cancer, openly showing scars where breasts once were. I shared by showing my port implant scars. We laughed, joked, and sometimes cried together. We shared our burdens and hugged each other. We also shared the pain, grief, and loss that cancer had caused us.

While some of us lost friends in the process, other friendships were strengthened or formed. We also shared the difficulties that friends and family had in understanding our suffering. They all expected us to feel and act normal and to do all we once did, not understanding that we had developed limitations—cancer had robbed us of "normal." These limitations were our "new" normal. We watched silently as some lost hair and then applauded with excitement as they grew their hair back. We watched as pale faces regained their color after chemotherapy was completed. Cancer had taken its toll on all of us.

Tom returned by Angel Flight for Thanksgiving. After the holiday, I flew back to California with him for a week in between chemo treatments. When I arrived, I still remembered my way around the complex. My husband surprised me by having already decorated the apartment for Christmas—he had strung lights and set out candles, a festive plant, and wrapped gifts.

The next day I saw Brittney outside and called to her. She recognized my voice and called, "Patricia, I haven't seen you for so long." The next few days we visited, prayed, and she had me read the Twenty-Third Psalm and another chapter from First John. I also shared my cancer story with her. She said she'd be leaving soon to go back home to live with her parents. That saddened me since she was the only friend I had in California, and we were just getting to know each other. Since it was nearly Christmas, I bought her a purple stuffed Harmony Care Bear. The Care Bear had hearts on its feet and chest, and I placed her hands on them so she could feel those shapes. Then I described its purple color. She suddenly said she had something to show me and brought out a singing purple doll with a matching purple hat given to her by a friend. She set them side-by-side on the coffee table, and they were a matching pair! Then I said a tearful good-bye, not knowing if we'd ever meet up with each other again. We were two people brought together by circumstances of disability. The friend I offered to take under my wing was vanishing forever from my life, or so I thought. I gulped, since I knew she couldn't see the tears as I wiped my eyes with the back of my hand.

That Sunday, Tom and I attended church, where Christmas decorations were set out for those in attendance to participate in decorating the tree. I found an angel and placed it high on the treetop for Tom to see and be reminded of me after I returned to Santa Fe. Then we went to a Christmas party at his workplace, where they had Hawaiian dancers. My heart ached for a chance to go on a trip to visit far-off Hawaii.

Then began my long Angel Flight home. It took four different flights to get back to Santa Fe this time. On the third flight, I flew with Todd, who had piloted my very first Angel Flight. As I updated him about the book I was writing, he asked, "What book? You didn't tell me about a book!" I realized I hadn't told him about writing my cancer story. Then I learned that he was a publisher and willing to publish my book. God had again answered my prayers.

On the fourth Angel Flight segment, the plane's lights began flickering on and off well before we reached Albuquerque. The pilot looked worried and said, "Oh no." It was pitch-black outside, and the pilot tried to radio the control tower but discovered that we had lost all communications. The only electricity working on the plane was wingtip lights. Since the pilot was concerned that other planes wouldn't know our location, he decided upon an emergency landing in Albuquerque. The plane lost altitude immediately, and I asked the pilot if he was lowering the plane himself. "Yes," he reassured me. "Even with electrical failure, planes can still safely land." Anxiously, I waited for a flicker of light or a voice from the radio, but all I heard was static and then complete silence. It was the longest forty-five minutes of my life! Feeling that I must help somehow, I placed my hand on the control panel and prayed. The pilot was alarmed and asked me what I was doing. I said, "Just praying," and then realized that I shouldn't touch those controls! As the lights continued flickering on and off, I peacefully knew we'd land safely. Upon landing we discovered that enough of our distress message had gotten through to the control tower, so they had turned up the brightness of the runway lights, the only beacon we had in a huge city. God again was merciful.

The pilot had parked his car at the airport, so after we called our families, he drove me to Santa Fe. He told me that this was the first time he had ever experienced trouble with his plane. I told him that I knew it wasn't my time yet and it wasn't his time either. When we arrived in Santa Fe, I asked what his favorite cookie was and found that it was oatmeal. So once again I did my "cookie care package thing."

Once I was safely in bed, I suffered all night from stomachaches and felt extremely nauseous by morning. In the shower, I vomited. I was scheduled for chemo the next day but instead was given IVs for nausea and to replace my lost fluids. I was diagnosed with the flu and was sick the remainder of the week. My chemo treatment was postponed until the following week.

In mid-December, Tom returned for our first Christmas together since his transfer. While he was home, my ninth chemo was the worst of the series. We had lots of snow the day before, and it was bitter cold. I developed severe pain, nausea, and even tongue blisters from the treatment and spent most of the time in bed. A week and a half later, however, my health improved enough to allow our family to have a beautiful Christmas together. The next day I learned that my CA 125 count had dropped to 4, so I celebrated by baking pumpkin pies and a turkey dinner. The following day, two feet of snow fell and we were snowbound. Thank God for leftover turkey. His timing was perfect again.

The 1000-Mile Odyssey

This is a story about five guys, four airplanes, planning, execution, and the great Angel Flight West (AFW) staff who somehow manage to coordinate everything and everybody involved. This story is dedicated to Patricia Santistevan, a cancer patient and an AFW passenger.

Patricia and her husband Thomas lived near Santa Fe, NM. She is currently receiving cancer treatment in Santa Fe, NM. Thomas is currently stationed near San Pablo, CA. That is one heck of a commute by anyone's standards. Thomas is an active

member of our US Army, and I am very happy that he got to visit her in NM over the Thanksgiving weekend. AFW put together this four-leg flight to get him home to California again on Sunday, November 25, 2007.

The whole trip experienced by Thomas on Sunday 11-25-2007 extended over 914 nm or 1051 miles. The other four participants in the day's activities have generously decided to participate in telling this story. The pilot who flew the first leg is John Courtright. The pilot who flew the second leg is Todd Underwood along with his young sons. I flew the third leg. The pilot who flew the fourth and longest leg is John Birely along with his son and Mission Assistant, Paul. Our passenger that day was Thomas Santistevan. Here are our recollections about the day.

The First Leg

It was clear and about 24 degrees in Albuquerque at 6:10 MST when I got up to start the first leg of the mission to take Thomas from Santa Fe, "The City Different," to Oakland. Winds were light at the Sunport when I took off in N64307, my 1975 C-172M to go the 60 miles to Santa Fe. Winds were 17G27 as I approached, favoring RWY 33 with its 0.7% upgrade. I had time for a cup of coffee at the Air Center FBO before Thomas and Patricia arrived. Patricia told me she was sending cupcakes along for the pilots.

Tom and I departed about 9:10 MST, climbed 4,200 feet to 10,500, set the GPS and autopilot, for Saint John's Industrial Airpark, AZ, and settled into a relatively smooth flight. A half hour later, we passed just to the north of the Acoma Pueblo, the oldest continuously occupied community in the US. After that we passed over a lava field, spreading south and west of Mount Taylor, and farmhouses in western New Mexico, we saw the steam rising from the power generator plant 10 miles from St John's airport. We landed in calm winds about 10:50 MST and pulled up to the FBO, to get fuel and await the arrival of Todd Underwood, the second leg pilot, about 10 minutes later. My return trip to the Albuquerque Sunport was uneventful. By John Courtright.

The Second Leg

I woke up early to a cold and clear Sunday morning in Prescott, AZ, but somehow the kids had still managed to get up earlier than I did. They knew we were going on an Angel Flight, and they were excited as they always are on Angel Flight mission days. We left early for the airport in order to make sure our 1966 PA-260B (Piper Comanche) was ready to go as it had just received a new engine. As I fired up the engine, the kids warmed up the headsets for our flight to St. Johns, AZ where we would be picking up Angel Flight passenger Thomas Santistevan. Thomas is a "repeat" customer, and we have flown both him and his wife, Patricia, many times. In fact, we flew this exact flight last year at the same time to the same place to get Thomas home to be with his family for the Thanksgiving holiday. It would be good to see him again. Thomas and Patricia have three sons just as my wife and I do, and I often ask Thomas for advice. Our flight to St. John's was pleasant and uneventful and we made it in less than an hour, averaging over 170kts.

About 20 miles out I heard the first leg pilot, John Courtright, call on the radio that he was downwind for 32. John and I have been splitting Angel Flight missions at the St. John's airport for about a year and a half now, and he is a really great guy with a big heart for our patients. We landed right behind him and both John and Thomas were there to meet us. After the usual enjoyable airport banter Thomas gave each of us, even the kids, a homemade cupcake baked for the pilots by his wife, Patricia. They were fantastic—filled with fruit and goodness, and the kids ate every last bite. After paying for our discounted fuel (thanks to Gary, the airport manager at St. John's!) and biding our adieus, Thomas, the kids, and I took off into the still below freezing air en route to Phoenix Deer Valley airport where we would meet up with the next leg pilot Ed Shreffler. Our flight was smooth as could be, and the visibility was excellent. At one point we could see the San Francisco peaks near Flagstaff, the New Mexico border behind us, the Superstition Mountains to the south of us, and the Four Peaks in front of us all at the same time. If you have never flown in Arizona you are really missing out!

As we arrived at Deer Valley airport, the busiest general aviation airport in the United States two years running, the controllers were doing an excellent job of keeping the traffic flowing on this Sunday after Thanksgiving. With no delays we landed and exited onto the taxiway with a smiling and waving Ed Shreffler and his Mooney. As we deplaned Ed came right over eager to shake hands and clearly excited about today's Angel Flight. Ed's son-in-law Darrin took pictures of all of us just before eating one of Patricia's cupcakes. Darrin had previously prepared lunch for Thomas as they knew he would be hungry during this all-day event. After moving Thomas's bags to Ed's plane, we said our goodbyes and took off again for our short flight home back to Prescott. We put the plane away but left it semi-prepared for another Angel Flight mission the following day. There is nothing more rewarding the flying for Angel Flight and being able to take part in the transportation of our patients who might not otherwise be able to get the medical treatment they so badly need. —*By Todd Underwood*

The Third Leg

I woke up a half an hour early because my subconscious was on special flight alert. Perfect blue sky was my good fortune. Both runwayfinder.com and wunderground.com gave me the total weather picture. Three cups of coffee later, Todd called and gave me a planned 12:20 arrival time. I called John Birely and gave him an update on my arrival time in Corona. Darrin made two awesome turkey sandwiches for us to enjoy in flight. I hugged my daughter goodbye, and we were off to the airport.

We got to Deer Valley and I called Flight Service to confirm the weather and all was good to go while Darrin was out on the ramp pre-flighting 07T. Once outside, I saw Todd taxiing his Comanche and waved him to a parking spot right next to us.

Cupcakes, can you believe it? Mine was awesome at 8,500 feet! The flight itself was a non-event. Smooth as sitting on a living room couch and George [the King KFC 150 autopilot] was flying. The altitude-hold feature kept us within 10 feet of 8500 feet for almost two hours. I could never do that manually. ATC sure was busy. I put us down on the centerline at Corona, and taxied to my hangar. Thomas and I pushed 5807T up the rise into her hangar and we drove over to transient parking. There we met John Birely and his son Paul.

Soon, they were off for Oakland. I tidied up the hangar, made friends with a Blue Can, reflected on the day, and went home to start writing this and become an all-around pest to get the other guys to do the same. —*By Ed Shreffler*

The Fourth Leg

I was pleased to accept the fourth and final leg of AF Mission #140552 for Thomas Santistevan on Sunday, November 25, 2007 from Corona, CA (KAJO) to Oakland, CA (KOAK). Thomas, his wife, Patricia, and I had flown together before, so that I knew what a great guy Thomas is. It was a privilege to fly a member of the US Army who serves our country with pride and commitment.

The day started with the usual questions. Would the weather allow each of the four legs to be flown safely? Would I be fit to fly my leg? Would I find my airplane, a 2004 turbocharged Cessna T182T with tail number N65377, to be airworthy when I arrived at my home base, Buchanan Field in Concord, CA (KCCR)? Perhaps the most unique thing about this mission for me was that my son Paul, who had recently moved from the East Coast to live with me in Oakland, would be flying his first Angel Flight as my mission assistant. As Paul is attempting to enlist in the Army, he was looking forward to meeting an active duty soldier.

Everything looked good on our weather briefing. In particular, Santa Ana winds led to better than usual visibility in the Los Angeles basin. Although the weather looked good for a VFR flight, we filed an IFR flight plan and received an IFR clearance that Paul and I flew upon departure from KCCR. For once, Murphy's Law of Aviation—that the wind is always in your face—wasn't operative, and we had a faster than planned flight to KAJO. Owing to heavy traffic and realizing that KAJO was clearly in VFR conditions, we cancelled our IFR clearance about 10 miles from KAJO to the delight of the overworked SOCAL Approach controller.

After the usual pit stop activities for Paul and me, and a quick refueling of N65377, we met up with Thomas and our third leg pilot and mission maestro Ed Shreffler. Thomas was his usual positive and energetic self, and surprised us with a cupcake that Patricia had baked. Paul snapped some pictures of Thomas, Ed, and me that came out great, and then it was time to fly to KOAK. Owing to good weather, we departed VFR. Although we had an IFR flight plan on file, we flew to KOAK with VFR flight following. Again, we had a smooth flight, with Thomas getting some sleep and no intervention of Murphy. Upon landing at KOAK, we taxied to the Kaiser Air FBO, which continued to be a great supporter of Angel Flight. Paul and I said farewell to an appreciative Thomas who drove home, and our mission ended with a quick, uneventful VFR hop from KOAK to KCCR.

This was a complex, four-leg mission that we executed as smoothly as could be hoped for. I look forward to flying Thomas and Patricia on future AF Missions, as well as to working with Ed and the other pilots who made the day such a success. *—By John Birely*

Our Passenger's Perception

The first pilot was John (Sorry I'm terrible at last names). I always enjoy flying with John. He seems to typify the warm kind-hearted father type figure or older brother who watches out for the younger brother. His plane is a two-seater Cessna, and when you get two big guys like him and me next to each other, we don't have much elbow room. Since it was a little cold when we left Santa Fe (I believe John said it was near 13 degrees), he asked me to pull on the knob for the heater whenever I noticed it going back in. I guess the force of the air pushing in through the nose of the plane kept closing the vent so we had to keep pulling it out. And since it was on the control panel in front of me, it was easier for me to pull. I felt it nice to be able to contribute a little to the flying of the plane if at least to make sure we had a nice warm supply of heat coming in. Because of the traffic over the airway, we didn't talk much except for a few words now and then as he had to continue to listen in and ensure that he heard any new instructions given to him to adjust altitude or direction for example.

We flew over a vast lava field from an ancient volcano south of Grants, New Mexico, just before we got to St. Johns, Arizona. It was amazing to see it from the air. We had a nice landing and were immediately greeted by Todd and his two younger sons. Getting down from the plane, we were happy to see the weather was a lot warmer than when we left Santa Fe. After going into the airport office there, I gave Todd and his two boys and John also, a cupcake each from the batch Patricia gave me. Her instructions were to make sure and give each of the pilots one to show our appreciation for flying me back to San Pablo, California.

The second pilot was Todd (same problem here—can't remember his last name). After we said bye to John, and everyone finished their cupcakes, we quickly boarded his plane and were on our way. His two boys sat in the rear seats. I always enjoy flying with Todd. He has three young sons, Gavin, Griffin, and I don't recall the name of the younger son. Patricia and I also have three sons, Joshua, Abraham, and Uriah. The first time I flew with Todd he told me how he and Patricia talked extensively, comparing notes on the upbringing of the boys, and it turned out we did the same. This last time however, and on the trip bringing me to Santa Fe, we talked quite a bit on experiences in the various churches we attended. It is so awesome because even three-four thousand feet up in the clouds, we could feel the presence of the Lord as we shared our mutual faith in Jesus.

The trip with Todd always goes by so quickly—not sure if it's because he flies so fast (Todd just put a new engine in his plane), or because time flies when you're having fun. His boys, lulled to sleep by the steady hum of the plane's engine (or being bored from our conversation), fell asleep in the back of the plane. They are so precious at that age. As always Todd enjoyed every minute with them while they are small—they grow up so quickly. We landed in Deer Valley airport in Phoenix and met up with Ed. After saying goodbye to Todd and loading up my bag in Ed's plane, we said goodbye.

The third pilot was Ed (hopefully by now you know I have no idea what his last name is). Ed is a really great guy. We got going after he made sure he had all the instructions and navigation items in place. He gave me a bag with a bottle of water, a delicious turkey sandwich, and a baggy with chips. Our conversation was mostly sparse, again due to the large Thanksgiving holiday traffic over the airways from everyone flying up there, but a few times we did get to talk about various things. I don't remember much about his plane. I think I was starting to get sleepy, and I believe a few times I kind of dozed off. When he opened his lunch, I did the same and we ate our picnic lunch on a blanket of clouds (no ants, ha-ha).

The trip went smoothly and again, seemed to pass very quickly. I remember the last part when we had to fly between two mountains to enter into the Los Angeles basin. He showed me on his instrument panel how the red portions indicated the mountains to our left and right that were equal to or above us, basically saying we did not want to get too close to them. We quickly began our descent; Ed flew in his approach angle, and we safely touched down in California. I had given the last two remaining cupcakes to Ed because when I first met him, I thought the gentleman next to him was also flying with us. Turned out he was just helping Ed get the plane ready to take off. So Ed gave me one of the cupcakes back to give to the next and last pilot of the final leg of my trip. When we landed, Ed asked me to help push his plane into the hangar, then we got in his SUV and drove around to the airport building where John and his son Paul were waiting for us. They talked for awhile and we said goodbye to Ed and boarded our plane.

The fourth pilot was John (not the same as the first John, and no I don't know his last name either). Guess I was pretty tired by this leg of the trip. I sat in the back, while John and Paul were up front. His plane had two large TV screen type monitors on the dashboard on the left and right. His son Paul helped him with the navigation, and John was careful to use the time as a training session to teach his son the important technical intricacies of flying. I really didn't talk to either of them while we were flying, but before getting on the plane, Paul told me he was talking to a recruiter and was definitely going to be joining the Army. He sounded pretty excited about it and reminded me of my years as a recruiter when I had an applicant join at MEPS. Sometimes they were a little scared, but most of the time they were excited at their decision and the job they got in the Army. We saw the most beautiful sunset from the plane, and as it grew dark, it seemed to get a lot colder up there. Fortunately, I had my thicker jacket in the bag and was able to reach it behind me. I snuggled into the warm fleece lining, closed my eyes, and fell asleep.

I awoke as we were nearing Oakland. John and Paul were both

watching out for about three or four different planes at one time that they received warnings from that they may be flying below us and or being near to intersecting our paths. Nothing to worry about, but they notified the dispatcher whenever they saw one of the planes. We landed safely in Oakland, and I said goodbye to John and Paul as they had to get back in their plane to fly to Concord. John said it would take them about 15-20 minutes to get there.

The fifth pilot was Tom. Well, I made it to my car, my little flyer Subaru WRX STI, that drove me the 15 miles or so north of Oakland up I-80 to San Pablo, CA. It was a long day of flying, but I made it safely home. I had four wonderful flights with four different and very special pilots. Words cannot express the thanks both Patricia and I and my family (my 93-year-old mother came and spent Thanksgiving with us) have for all of you. In spite of all that Patricia has gone through, she remains in high spirits. Being apart from her has been difficult for both her and me. Right now, I'm in the process of requesting a compassionate reassignment back to New Mexico to be near to my beautiful wife as she continues the struggle for life in her battle with cancer. But for now, the year and four months I've been out here, being so far hasn't felt so far thanks to Angel Flight and all its wonderful people who contribute to providing such an honored, needed, and very appreciated service. May God bless all of you who make this happen. Thanks again to all you special pilots who take the time to fly us safely to our destinations and to be with our loved ones. May God richly bless you now and always!

Sincerely,
Tom Santistevan,
SFC Thomas L. Santistevan

Chapter 10

Mountains Moving

My tenth chemo treatment came on January 3, 2007, and left me almost as ill as the ninth. I again had three days of injections to boost my red and white blood cells. Usually following red blood cell injections, I would have an energy rush, but this time I felt severe morning pain and my arms felt like they'd fall off. My entire body hurt. I took 800 mg of Motrin and spent a lot of time in bed. I was so nauseated that all I could manage to eat was yogurt and a few snacks. My neck and throat hurt so much that I could hardly swallow. My nausea was nonstop, and all that my tired body and mind wanted was a final end to the chemotherapy. Throughout all this I stayed busy to distract myself from the painful ordeal. At night I prayed for God's release from this illness, but I also thanked Him for every good moment I had. Nevertheless, I mostly prayed for others so I wouldn't dwell upon myself.

After the holiday, Tom's car unexpectedly needed a new clutch, and he was unable to drive back to California. So he stayed an additional week while it was being repaired. The day that the repairs were completed, I barely choked back tears as I watched him drive off. I knew that if I started to cry, it would not be easy to stop. I swallowed hard and immediately got busy with the chores to keep me from breaking down emotionally. I managed to distract myself to keep from feeling the pain and agony in my heart. I felt only God understood the agony I was going through, so again I trusted in His help.

On January 10, I had my eleventh chemo treatment. Still nauseated when I saw Dr. Greenfield I asked, "Must I have this chemo?"

"Absolutely!" he replied. So I reminded him that he promised when my chemo began to either end chemo sooner or go longer.

I said, "Forget longer, and end sooner!"

He said, "Okay, for now."

I replied, "No! Forever. I don't ever want to go through any more chemo." I couldn't hold back the tears as my emotions surfaced, and I felt a sick feeling in the pit of my stomach at the thought of going through even one more treatment.

I was so relieved to finally end chemotherapy. I didn't have number twelve. Yet I was discouraged because I knew that there was no known cure for my cancer. Although I wanted Dr. Greenfield's expression of faith for a cure, I had enough faith for both of us, and faith the size of a mustard seed can move mountains.

Finally, Dr. Greenfield and I discussed a concrete future. He predicted that I had one to three years left to live. Although my current CA 125 reading was a 3, his prognosis was that the cancer would come back. Nevertheless I have kept the faith and traveled to and from California. Each day is a precious part of that mountain-moving as energy returned and I continued to feel better.

In March I flew to California in time for Tom's birthday. I cooked him his favorite meal and baked a cake to celebrate. We had a wonderful day together. I saw Brittney once more as she had come back to continue with school. However, this time she had a boyfriend and was too busy to spend time with me. While doing laundry, I met Brittney's roommate, Jennifer, and Jennifer's seeing-eye dog and made some new friends.

Tom was sent on work-related travel, and I was left alone in California for five days. So I called a past co-worker, who now lived in Reno, and asked if she would stay with me. She immediately drove to San Pablo (where our apartment is) and spent the five days with me. We shopped, walked along the bay, and took the BART to Chinatown in San Francisco.

After another month in California, I again said good-bye to Tom and took a commercial flight back to New Mexico. We celebrated the birthday of my oldest son, who turned twenty-six, along with my forty-ninth birthday. In mid-April I had my CA 125 blood test, and it went up to 5. Although it was low, I worried that it might continue rising and desperately prayed for God's healing. A week later, a CAT scan revealed that the nodule on my spleen was smaller and everything else was normal. At my mid-May appointment with Dr. Pardue, he again commented on how well I was doing, considering all that I had experienced. I continued to keep busy but became extremely fatigued. My body ached to a point that I had to take 800 mg of Motrin for pain. So I reduced my activity level, rested more, and my energy returned.

In May we celebrated my second son's twenty-fifth birthday. My youngest son would turn twenty-four in September. It was comforting to have my three sons with me while Tom lived in California. We prayed for the day we'd all be together again.

A Walk of Faith

In June 2007, Tom flew home and we celebrated our twenty-eighth wedding anniversary by having dinner and staying at the Marriott in Albuquerque. That weekend I attended a writing workshop at the cancer institute. Here are a few of my writings:

Nightfall

Oh the night falls and I welcome it. How did I get here; when did I get here? In the dark I feel the agony, the pain, the loneliness. My body shakes as tears fill my eyes. This time I can't hold them back. My husband holds my hand, oh how comforting. My Jesus is close to me; my angels surround me. I feel, I feel the prayers.

As the night falls, I pray, oh God! Deliver me, set me free.

Bring healing. Help me with the pain, the anguish. Loss of hair, loss of body parts. How did all this happen? What did I do? I tried so hard to live according to God's will, but did I fail? No, I was chosen, chosen to live a path unknown to me. Chosen for a reason.

Quietly I listen, the chimes, the wind, the crickets. It all seems so strange. I feel so alone. The darkness envelops me. I lie awake. Eyes round as saucers. When will sleep come? I can't lie still. I think, I wonder, I pray. Finally I sleep. So exhausted, I wake, can't move, it hurts to get up. I need help, I need water, I need someone to take this all away. Relief, freedom, strength, I must, I must survive this…

My Favorite Meal

My favorite meal is with the family around the table. My husband next to me and my three sons around me. Flowers in the center and candles softly glowing. The conversation smooth and flowing. The food carefully prepared and adorned with sweet-smelling spices. Aromas fill the air; laughter resounds everywhere.

Prayer sets off the meal. Sharing and honesty openly discussed. The lights are dim, the music is quiet and goes with the occasion. The door is open and the birds are happily chirping. How wonderful to be surrounded by family and feel the love and joyous laughter. Each and every meal is made special with someone to share it with.

Dear Patricia,

You didn't know. Even though you didn't feel well, you tried your best to look well. You tried to hold back the pain. To hide the bloated stomach. With sword in sheath you didn't know a battle was about to begin. A battle with cancer. Surgery and chemo were far from your mind. Not once did the thought occur that it could be cancer.

You did all the normal things: cook, clean, shop. You were

there for your family when they needed you. All day long you kept going, didn't stop, went to bed exhausted and wondering, why do I feel this way? What's wrong with me? When will all this end and I will get relief from this rut of living day in and day out? No time for yourself, too busy.

You tried to be there for everyone but yourself. You did for everyone and neglected yourself. But you kept going, kept fighting. Brushed all the problems to the back of your mind and still smiled for the world. No one knew, no one understood what you were going through. Only you felt the pain and emotion of it all.

Brain Wipe

"Chemo brain," a series of repeating myself and not knowing why. Things happened so fast. Could not remember the important things. Could not remember the faces. It's as if my memory was temporarily erased and then came back.

How long will I feel this way? How long before I feel normal again, like it used to be? Lists for everything from appointments to grocery shopping. Lists for chores and when it's time to water the plants. My poor dog, I wonder what he thinks…did I give him a dog treat already or has he had more than ten? I bet he likes the latter. Did I forget to put him out or let him in? He always reminds me.

My husband and sons are my second brain. Remind me, I tell them. I put this item there and that paper here. If they don't listen and remind me, oh well, I suppose someday I'll find it. Things misplaced but don't know where! Still can't find it. Every time I rearrange I forget where I put it. I guess I'll have to make a road map, put arrows and color-coordinate everything.

Some things my body reminds me of, like when to eat and drink. Notes, notes everywhere. Sticky notes here and sticky notes there. Now where is the notepad? Every few months, it's like Christmas again. Oh! I didn't know I had that. Surprises everywhere. Open the pantry and find the box of food I forgot to fix for dinner so I bought another one.

Inventory several times a year or how else will I know what to shop for? Write it down. Organize it and tell my family: "Don't touch that pantry!" If it all gets mixed up, I have to organize it again so I know exactly where everything is. Clean out the refrigerator or I won't find it. Where did I put it, oh poor me, not again, oh, there it is!

Cancer Recovery Brings Out the Kid in Me

Oh to be a child again, so happy and carefree. No bills to worry about. No housekeeping or problems. To let the wind blow back my hair and dance in the rain. To throw my hands up and spin in circles around the yard. To dance throughout the house and sing songs of praise.

To swing on the swing, lie on the grassy ground, and watch the sky as the hours go by. To splash in the water as laughter fills the air. Blow bubbles and watch them float away in rainbow colors. I try to catch them as the bubbles pop in my hand. One tickles as it lands on my nose. Oh how fun to be a child again and not feel silly doing the hula-hoop in my back porch.

At this time Tom's sister was very ill with cancer, and we took her to the doctor in Albuquerque. He told us she had only six months left to live because the chemotherapy was no longer working. Tragically, one week later she passed away. Tom had just flown back to California. We contacted the Red Cross about his sister's condition, and the next day he flew back home. Between drives to Albuquerque and Taos for the funeral, Tom and I were both exhausted.

On June 27, bright and early, Tom and I took the long Angel Flight back to California. We were blessed with a six-seater plane this time, giving me room to lie down in the backseat. We both fell sound asleep. We only had to change planes twice to reach California this time. Tom and I spent the Fourth of July in San Francisco, walking to Chinatown and back to Fisherman's Wharf to watch the fireworks. The splendor of seeing fireworks reflected in the water below us was spectacular, like nothing I had ever seen before. It was truly amazing and a beautiful sight to behold. Then it was back to walks by the bay and local shopping trips. One weekend we drove across the San Mateo Bridge to Half-Moon Bay and took U.S. Highway One to Pacifica and the beach. The following weekend we went to the Japanese Tea Gardens, Botanical and Rose Gardens, finishing up with an evening meal at the Mozart Restaurant, the most romantic restaurant in California.

On Wednesday we went wading in the sandy bay at Pinole Shores. That Friday, July 20, there was a 4.42 magnitude earthquake at 4:42 a.m. in the Richmond Fault Line. There were broken windows in the nearby Safeway in Berkley; wine bottles crashed to the floor, and the store was closed down. I heard rumbling, a loud crash, and a boom, boom sound. I thought they were gunshots in the building next door. I went back to sleep and upon awakening that morning, Tom turned my attention to the news on TV, talking about the earthquake that was felt everywhere in the area. Tom said that he had actually felt the bed move and the wall creak. I was half-packed for my Angel Flight back to Santa Fe the next day. The earthquake had made me very nervous and a little frightened, so I was very relieved to be flying out the next day. However, I hated to leave my husband behind and wished that he could come with me. At 1:12 a.m. that night I felt an aftershock, again with the same sounds but not as loud. At 7 a.m. I kissed and hugged my husband good-bye as I climbed aboard the small plane. I arrived in Santa Fe at 6 p.m., glad to be home sound and safe.

In August when I was tested and found positive for the BRCA1 gene mutation, my worst fears were realized. This news meant that my parents, brothers and sisters, and sons had up to a

50 percent chance of carrying the same mutation. Other relatives might also be at risk of having it. Genetic testing is the only way to accurately identify mutation carriers. Having the carriers puts them at a higher risk of developing some form of cancer: an 87 percent risk of developing breast cancer and a 44 percent risk of ovarian cancer by age seventy in women. Mutations in BRCA1 have been reported to confer a 20 percent risk of a second breast cancer within five years of the first, as well as a tenfold increase in the risk of subsequent ovarian cancer. This mutation may also confer an increased (albeit low) risk of male breast cancer, as well as some other cancers. This explained my frequent cancer recurrences. My maternal aunt also tested positive for the deleterious mutation. The mutation was passed down generationally from my grandfather to my mother to me.

Knowing this critical information much earlier could have helped me avoid a late diagnosis. I was the first one as far as I know to be tested for the BRCA1 and 2 sequencing tests in my family. This information will help my sisters and any future granddaughters to go for frequent checkups to catch any signs of cancer early, perhaps taking drugs like Tamoxifen to reduce their risks. Oral contraceptives may also reduce the risk of ovarian cancer in women with BRCA1 or BRCA2 mutations. Knowing leaves room for surgical choices, but it also means living with uncertainty and worrying over every ache and lump. Knowing also prompts those diagnosed with these mutations to eat the world's healthiest diet, religiously avoiding refined sugar of any kind as well as refined carbohydrates and any other artificial food. Exercise is also extremely important for people with BRCA 1 and 2 mutations.

On the first of August, I had my usual CA 125 test, which was a 9. Tom drove to Santa Fe in time for his mother's birthday, and I went back with him to California. This time we drove to Sausalito and walked across the Golden Gate Bridge, which is 1.7 miles across to San Francisco. It took us about two hours to walk it. I felt that this was an opportunity of a lifetime, and I didn't know if I would be able to do it at any other time so I jumped at the opportunity. It was exhilarating to feel the bridge under my feet, and the view was awesome. Back at the apartment I made a new friend, Kevin, who had been blind for three years. I baked some oatmeal cookies for him, and we chatted and I prayed for him. I then prepared for another Angel Flight back to Santa Fe. This time we had turbulence and needed to land in Prescott, Arizona, where I stayed overnight with Todd's family and took the next-day Angel Flight back to Santa Fe. I was pleased to meet Todd's wife and his three sons who are close in age as are my three sons, so we had something in common.

My CA 125 in September was a 13, and a PET scan revealed cancer on the spleen, pelvis, and abdomen. I again prepared for more chemo, this time with the drug Doxil. Despite this news, I again volunteered for registration and exhibit room duty at another Glorieta Cancer Retreat. This time I attended the retreat alone. After my first chemo treatment, I attended a women's retreat with our churchwomen in Taos. Not feeling well, I required a lot of rest but enjoyed myself. Back home I resumed my usual routine, attending cancer support groups and walking with Krypto. I acquired a new dog, Ashley, a Dachshund-Chihuahua mix, as a mate for Krypto. Ashley was three years old. However, after just six months she unexpectedly passed away. Again I grieved another loss but was thankful I still had Krypto.

October brought a series of tests and more chemo. A breast MRI, mammogram, and ultrasound for a spot on my left breast revealed no cancer. However, the CA 125 reading continued to rise to 18.

I prepared for a commercial flight back to Oakland. During my two weeks with Tom, I was plagued by neuropathy on my hands, which were irritated, red, and swollen. (Neuropathy, also called hand and foot syndrome, involves tingling, numbness, burning sensations, or just plain pain. It's a pins-and-needles sensation in fingers and toes alike.) I also had severe blisters on my tongue and a rash under my arms and on my legs. I called Dr. Lopez for more prescriptions to ease the symptoms. The pain was so great that just trying to talk, chew, or swallow brought me to tears. A week later, Tom and I went to Jack London Square and took a ferry to San Francisco and a fishing boat cruise under the Golden Gate Bridge and around Alcatraz. Overall it was relaxing and my time with Tom ended all too quickly. I flew back home for another CA 125, which was back down to 5. Therefore, the doctor was able to reduce the dosage on my next chemo treatment.

Anticipating the coming Thanksgiving holiday, I again prayed for strength and help to bake pies and muffins. With the help of two teenage girls from church, God answered my prayers, and we baked thirteen pumpkin pies from two fresh pumpkins and four apple pies from fresh apples. I also baked four dozen Bran Flax muffins from scratch. Some of these were for the Angel Flight pilots. I also made Thanksgiving dinner for my husband, his mother, and my three sons. Tom came home on an Angel Flight just in time for the Thanksgiving weekend.

After Tom returned to California, I had another CA 125 test. This time it was between 0 and 1! Another miracle. Dr. Greenfield had never expected it to go back down to even a 3. By this time, Dr. Greenfield had retired and my new oncologist was Dr. Lopez.

My fourth chemo treatment brought fatigue, irritated and hurting hands, and blisters under my tongue, though not as bad as they were previously. I was unable to type or write because of the pain in my hands, and by this time, I was desperately praying for a dishwasher and help around the house.

In December, the women from church and I baked cookies and distributed them to nursing homes and sang Christmas carols. My sons helped me bake biscochitos. I went to the River of Lights display in Albuquerque with a church group and the next day I experienced horrible pain and soreness in my body. I recuperated just in time for Tom's homecoming for the holiday.

Another CA 125 test was a 3. We spent Christmas with our family in Taos and, after the New Year, Tom returned to California. Dr. Lopez again reduced the dosage on my next chemo treatment because of the profound side affects I was experiencing.

On February 1, 2008, I took another commercial flight to visit Tom. We spent Valentine's Day together at a nice French restaurant. Tom helped me bake cookies to take to his workplace. I continued to experience lower back pain and fatigue. After sixteen days in California, I returned home for another CA 125 test. It still looked good at a 4, and I finished up with the sixth chemo on February 28.

By March I was participating in the Gilda Radner Ovarian Cancer research study, which is in Roswell, New Mexico. On the twenty-eighth, the PET scan revealed a complete resolution. No more cancer! The doctors told me that I had beaten the odds. One of them even said that "someone from above" was intervening for me. None of them expected me to go into another remission. God does answer prayer.

I found a free dishwasher at a yard sale and a member from my church helped with the plumbing for it. However, after installing it we found that it leaked. A couple of weeks later, I found a new dishwasher at a wholesale price. God had been preparing me this entire time for His very best. Isn't He good?!

On April 4, my CA 125 remained at 4, and God brought a very lovely family into my life to help me clean the house. They enabled me to conserve energy and work on this manuscript. Meanwhile, I had remodeled the kitchen and bathrooms, with some help, of course. I was taking the Tamoxifen pill (a hormone inhibitor) to keep me in remission. But God has been my ultimate source of strength and healing. On May 27, another CA 125 was a 5.

Chapter 11

Keep on Trusting

On June 30, 2008, a stomach virus landed me in the ER with severe cramping and diarrhea. Thankfully, a series of tests and a CAT scan revealed no cancer. Tom was home at the time for two weeks to spend the Fourth of July with us.

By this time Dr. Pardue was no longer my doctor; my new oncologist surgeon was Dr. Muller and my primary doctor was Dr. Serendowych. On July 8, I was diagnosed with osteopenia and arthritis in my lower spine by Dr. Serendowych and put on the once-a-week pill Fosamax. Since my original diagnosis I had already shrunk a half inch in height. However, after only six months of taking Fosamax, I shrank another half inch! The pill initially made me so groggy that I couldn't wake up in the morning. It was as if I had taken a strong sleeping pill. I just couldn't open my eyes and for several days slept all morning! I felt extremely fatigued, and every bone in my body ached to a point of requiring me to take 800 mg of Motrin to ease the pain. Eventually my body got used to it and I felt better, but some fatigue and aching persisted. Six months later, Dr. Serendowych took me off Fosamax, and I bounced back.

August brought green chili roasting and freezing as well as baking some ten-day Amish friendship breads to freeze for the holidays. I went into a baking frenzy, baking fourteen loaves of Amish bread! I even baked a cake for my mother-in-law's ninety-fourth birthday. On August 25, another CA 125 was a 7.

Tom flew home for the Labor Day weekend, which ended all

too quickly. After his departure I went to Grants, New Mexico, with my aunt and uncle for a very relaxing week. I returned home to more green chili roasting and freezing and making of red chili caribe for freezing. I even made a chili ristra.

In September, my friend Sophie and I went to Dixon Ranch for apples, waiting in a seven-mile line of traffic for three hours! (I don't believe I'll do that again.) With the Dixon Ranch apples, I went on an apple-pie baking frenzy, baking six apple pies and freezing two of them for when Tom came home for the holidays. Tom's favorite pie is apple. I dehydrated the rest of the apples. Later I baked four zucchini breads. I was well prepared for the holidays and company, giving Amish bread away and being ready for that last-minute potluck.

It had been a very busy summer and fall indeed and, as usual, the holidays came all too quickly. I helped two friends move. And I watched and cried as my dear friend Therese passed away, and I lost an aunt to cancer. My burden continued to grow as my cousin Nancy was diagnosed with breast cancer, underwent surgery and chemotherapy, and lost her brother to diabetes while her mother (my Aunt Susie) continued her own battle with ovarian cancer. Aunt Susie is my mom's sister and, like myself, was tested positive for hereditary cancer.

When my dear friend Diane went to a nursing home, I visited and prayed with her. When she moved to Florida, it was difficult holding back the tears as my emotions took over and sadness overwhelmed me. I loved Diane as my own sister and continue to miss her terribly.

Too much, too quickly! I felt useful as I tried my best despite my own struggles and limitations to be there for others to help and encourage them. There were times I became so fatigued that I needed to slow down and rest. As people disappeared from my life, I felt frustrated and useless, but I knew God would bring more people my way. As I focused on the needs of others, my own struggles seemed far away. I kept myself so busy to keep from feeling the loneliness deep inside. I tried to volunteer at nursing homes, but then it happened again…

On November 20, my CA 125 went up to 17, more than double from the last one. I knew this was not a good sign. I feared cancer's recurrence but kept my hopes up and prayers going for complete healing. I was not feeling well, the fatigue was increasing, and the aching in my abdomen and pelvic area was persistent. Nonetheless I had family over for Thanksgiving dinner. I managed to bake four pumpkin pies from scratch, made cranberry relish, and baked the turkey and fixings. I managed a last-minute flight for Tom with the generous help of a couple from church who had been giving us free flights since Tom's move.

Tom flew in on Thanksgiving Day just in time for dinner. I had decorated the house and quickly changed into a flashing red top and freshened up my makeup as I rushed to the door to welcome him home for the holiday. Sadly, his visit lasted only three days. Tom flew back to Oakland very early Sunday morning, but not before our youngest son, Uriah, announced his engagement to a beautiful young lady. Now I had a wedding to prepare for. The anticipation was too much as I kept asking Uriah when the Big Day would be. Finally my dreams were coming true for me to see my sons get married. I looked forward with much excitement to the wedding and grandchildren in the future. My future looked bright and hopeful.

On December first, my mother had hip replacement surgery. I told her that I would go to Taos to help her after the surgery, not knowing that another battle was fast approaching for me. I visited her in the hospital and became ill after only four hours there. I felt dizzy, weak, and tired, so I retreated outdoors for some much-needed fresh air. Feeling better, I went back to the ICU to tell my mother that I wouldn't be back to visit because of the symptoms I continually get when I'm in hospitals. With tears, I left the hospital and my mother to the care of doctors and my sisters who were visiting her.

Back home I was scheduled for a PET scan and another CA 125, which rose to 20 from the 17 on the test only twenty days prior. On December 16, 2008, I saw Dr. Lopez in his office at the Cancer Institute. Before he walked in I asked for a copy of the test results. As he walked in I was still holding the test results and reading it in disbelief. He asked if I knew what was happening. I whispered, "Yes." I couldn't hold back the tears as Dr. Lopez hugged me and expressed his sympathy. I gulped and swallowed hard as I knew what I needed to do.

That day we got a lot of snow and the roads were icy so there were many cancellations in the chemo suite. Dr. Lopez explained that I could begin chemotherapy immediately or wait until after the Christmas holiday. Knowing what my chances were, I made the decision to waste no time and began chemotherapy right away.

The cancer was in the same areas as it had been previously: in the pelvic area, outside the spleen, and in the abdomen. I was given the same chemo as before—Doxil. As I sat in the chair while the infusion was being administered through my port, I continued to hold the test results and read and reread them in hopes that there was some mistake and the results weren't mine. Finally, I relaxed, settled back, and closed my eyes. And so, the battle continued...

The next few weeks again brought nausea, weakness, and dizziness. My activity level slowed and I slept a lot. I experienced severe abdominal bloating and pain for an agonizing week. Finally I found relief, just in time for another chemo. The good news was the CA 125 dropped to 16, then again to 8 and back down to 5. The chemo was working. With unwavering faith I continued to trust God for healing and restoration.

Dr. Lopez spread out the chemo from four to five weeks to give me additional recovery time. I felt much better and energy returned. I hadn't felt this well in many years. With my newfound energy I worked in the garden, planting flowers and vegetables and enjoying the spring breezes. I acquired a new female puppy that brought joy and happiness into my life. I ended another session of six chemos, bringing the total to thirty-one in five years. However, my future remained in God's hands.

Since there is no cure for ovarian cancer, if I stopped chemo altogether, it would only be a matter of time before another occurrence. Dr. Lopez recommended a maintenance program of chemotherapy every two to three months for the rest of my life. As long as the chemo worked, I could maintain a good quality of life. However, once the body rejects all chemos, there is nothing to be done except wait at death's door. My prayer is for a cure to be found.

On April 19, 2009, my Aunt Susie passed away from ovarian cancer. Her ashes were buried at the foot of her son's grave. I had the opportunity to visit her on Easter weekend and pray with her. I knew it would be the last time I would see her. She was ready and at peace. I know God has kept me here all these years for a reason, and as I submit to God I believe He can use me to offer hope and encouragement to others just as others have done for me during my initial diagnosis and surgery. God has allowed me the opportunity to visit and pray with many others as they faced their struggles. My heart's desire is to help others facing the same struggles that I have endured. No matter what struggles you might be facing right now, remember that God has not given us a spirit of fear but of love, power, and a sound mind. He will help you get through whatever life throws at you because He loves you and cares about you. He will never give you more than you can handle. When you are ready, God will carry you through and take you on to new realms. Allow Him to carry you and be your ultimate source. Either way you will come out on the winning side if you will just put your total trust in Him.

Here are some encouraging words that have helped to sustain me in the most difficult of times.

"It is good for me that I have been afflicted, that I might learn thy statutes" (Psalm 119:71 KJV).

"God's strength is best seen in our weakness." Taken from *Our Daily Bread*, Jan. 12, 2009.

"I would tell the Lord my longings, roll on Him my every care; cast upon Him all my burdens, burdens that I cannot bear." Taken from *Our Daily Bread*, Jan. 14, 2009.

"I will speak in the anguish of my spirit" (Job 7:11 KJV).

"You can't keep misery from coming but you don't have to give it a chair to sit on." A proverb.

"For thou art my hope, O Lord GOD: thou art my trust from my youth" (Psalm 71:5 KJV).

"The Lord himself goes before you and will be with you; He will never leave you nor forsake you. Do not be afraid; do not be discouraged" (Deut. 31:8).

"Then you will know the truth, and the truth will set you free" (John 8:32).

"Into His hands I lay the fears that haunt me, the dread of future ills that may befall; into His hands I lay the doubts that taunt me, and rest securely, trusting Him for all." Taken from *Our Daily Bread*, Feb. 12, 2009.

"In all your ways acknowledge Him, and He shall direct your paths" (Prov. 3:6 KJV).

"Why are you cast down, O my soul? Hope in God, for I shall yet praise Him for the help of His countenance" (Psalm 42:5 KJV).

"When our lives are heavy laden, cold and bleak as winter long, stir the embers in our hearts, Lord; make your flame burn bright and strong." Taken from *Our Daily Bread,* Feb. 19, 2009.

"We all have a story to tell, but many of us don't realize that our difficulties and dilemmas, once we've had a degree of healing, can be used to encourage others." Taken from the book, *Behind the Personality,* by Florence Littauer.

Also by Florence: *"How exciting it was to see each woman realize she didn't need to be ashamed of her past, but she could use her victimization and victories as inspiration for others in similar circumstances. She could make her tough times really count!"*

"There is hope in your future" (Jer. 31:17).

Closing

I celebrated my fiftieth birthday on April 20, 2008, with flowers, balloons, and dinner with my family at Red Lobster. God has been good. Back in 2004, after my first chemo session and knowing what my chances of survival were, someone once asked me: "You're still here?" My answer was then and still is: "Yes, I'm still here, alive and well. Thanks to all your prayers."

As I reflect on these difficult years, I see God's handwriting on every page of my life. As my story unfolded, my life became richer, knowing that although cancer has repeatedly touched my life, I have become a better person. I have become more patient and have learned not to stress over little things in life. I have also developed a closer relationship with God. I have a new appreciation for life and a greater love for everyone. I now have confidence that, with God's help, I will get through this and whatever else life has in store for me.

I always look forward to spring every year. And just as the flowers bloom and take on bright, vibrant colors, so has my life taken on new meaning. As the colors come alive in spring, so have the colors of my life come alive. It is certain that my life will never be the same again. I am not the person I used to be. I have faced the losses, grief, and pain. Like a small bird that flies away and looks for new territory to dwell in and find shade, food, and water, so the Lord will help me find comfort in the shade, food to strengthen my body, and water to wash away the toxins and impurities in my body. As the Lord leads and guides me, I will face each day with a new boldness and renewed strength. I know that with God all things are possible, and He is in control of my future. Whatever burdens I have to bear in the New Year, I will bear with God's help, for He continually walks beside me.

God has assured me that "those who hope in the Lord will renew their strength. They will soar on wings like eagles; they will run and not grow weary, they will walk and not be faint" (Isaiah 40:31).

Appendix A: Tom's Story

Patricia was ill for quite some time prior to her diagnosis of cancer. She complained constantly of being bloated, especially when she ate. She could only eat small portions of food. The reason, of course, and one we didn't know, was that the ovarian cancer had gradually spread in her abdomen to the fatty tissue barrier of her lower diaphragm. Her abdominal cavity was full of fluid. It was so uncomfortable to eat. She got to the point where she dreaded sitting down to eat because she knew the unpleasant, uncomfortable pressure and nausea feeling she would encounter afterward.

It was hard for all of us (my boys and I) to see her this way. We felt so bad when we all sat at the table (it's been a family tradition for us to always try and share our meals together, especially dinner). As the rest of us were enjoying our meal, Patricia would be hurting and at times she'd even cry because she couldn't eat.

Her doctor kept trying to find what was wrong with her, attributing her illness to indigestion problems and even stress, but never considering the possibility that she might be seriously ill. The blood tests had no conclusive evidence to show that she was ill, so the doctor apparently didn't consider that she could have cancer.

Finally, because Patricia's condition grew worse, she was scheduled for a colonoscopy. I remember when Patricia told me that she had to go for this exam and that she would need someone to drive her. I knew then that, hopefully, we would now be able to get to the bottom of what was making her ill. When the doctor completed her exam, one of the nurses assisting the doctor told us the exam didn't show anything out of the ordinary. Patricia was still somewhat groggy from the medication she was given to undergo the test, so I told the nurse I didn't feel the results were correct or that maybe she may have some other illness that the test did not detect. She became somewhat upset at this and said we should be happy that her results were okay. We told her we were, but she didn't realize what Patricia was going through and that there had to be something seriously wrong with her.

Soon after that the doctor came to talk to us, and I told him that while we were glad she didn't have anything wrong in her colon region, this didn't mean that something wasn't seriously wrong with her. I tried to explain to him the symptoms she was having and afterward he said they would schedule an ultrasound. When they tried to do the test, they were not able to because of all the fluid in her abdomen around her organs (a sign of cancerous growth). They extracted the fluid and tested it to find that it did, indeed, contain cancerous growth. After they extracted much of the liquid, they were able to perform another ultrasound that gave an accurate picture, which led to a diagnosis of her ovarian cancer.

Thank the Lord for Dr. Pardue (he reminded me of my dad). He had the appearance and manner of the old kindhearted country doctor we trust and look to for hope and encouragement.

When Patricia came out of surgery, it was late; she was in there about an hour longer than she was supposed to be. The doctor came and talked to me first, along with Patricia's father. He said the cancer was well spread and that was why they took so long. He wanted to make sure he removed everything that could visibly be extracted surgically without having to cut into or remove portions of any major organs. The only part they had to remove other than her ovaries, fallopian tubes, and uterus, was the fatty layer of tissue that separated her upper and lower abdomen. I don't think they had to remove it all, just parts where the cancer was attached. He also said he cut a little into part of her gall bladder where it was attached, but was able to stitch it up properly, and she shouldn't have any complications as a result of that. He also said he was pleased that she didn't have any extensive growth embedded in her liver. What was visibly present he removed, and he believed he got it all.

What really struck me was what the doctor said had happened when they first opened her up. The doctor assisting him saw how extensive the cancer was and suggested maybe it was too far spread to effectively remove it all, and maybe they should just close her back up. But Dr. Pardue told me that he said at the time: "No, we can still get most of it and besides, we have to give her a fighting chance." I never forgot when he told me that.

Patricia was in postoperative care for another few hours before they released her to her room. When they brought her to the room, she was heavily sedated and recovering from the anesthesia in a partially unconscious state. As she came to and tried to see who was there in the room with her, she grasped my hand and asked me: "Tom, am I going to make it?" I tried to console her and tell her the surgery was very successful (as Dr. Pardue said, he did get all the major growths, and if they began chemotherapy while she was still in the hospital, it would start destroying the smaller growths that may have remained). But Patricia was very sedated, and I just tried to hold her hand to let her know I was still there. She asked me a second time if she was going to make it, and I told her she was going to be okay. For the remainder of that night, I stayed with her.

She couldn't have any water, but they allowed me to wet her lips with a moist sponge. I remembered the next day as she started getting better, she tried to squeeze the sponge with her lips in an attempt to get a few drops of water in her mouth. I've never felt so much compassion and felt so bad for anyone in my whole life as I did when I saw that. I remembered where the Lord talked about giving one of these little ones a drink in My name... I guess as she tried to squeeze out a few drops, I felt, "Oh well, a few drops won't hurt her." After the first day she was allowed to have a few ice chips. My dear Patricia loves to drink water, and as we went into the third day, I never saw anyone eat so many ice chips—poor thing.

The nursing staff put her in an extended special care room, part of the ICU, where she had a small chair that opened into a bed so I could stay with her.

Appendix B: Joshua's Story

On Christmas of 2003, my mom broke the news of her cancer. She told us that on her most recent visit to her doctor, ovarian cancer was detected in her pelvic area. At first, I couldn't believe what I was hearing. You always hear about cancer happening here and there: "Some movie star has cancer, breast cancer is on the rise, donate money to support cancer research, oh and you get to sign this balloon/shamrock/paper, and post it up on the window" in places you go, supermarkets, restaurants. But even though you give, even though you recognize that cancer is happening, you don't relate to it, you are disconnected from it, until something like this happens and it hits home.

At first I didn't comprehend what was happening. *Does this mean she is going to die?* I thought. My head was rushed with memories of my mom from my youth, from when my brothers and I were kids, and I realized that there might no longer be any more memories to be made. My dad mostly described exactly what was going on and when she was to be scheduled for surgery. Even today what was said that Christmas is still a blur. All I know is that I was scared, scared for her, scared that our family would lose a member and no longer be complete.

Appendix C: Abraham's Story

I remember when my mom was first diagnosed with her cancer. My initial reaction was that of shock. I didn't understand how her level of severity could have progressed so rapidly without anybody catching it earlier. I didn't even think about operations at first; all I knew was that my mom had a horrible disease and probably only a certain number of days to live.

The worst time was after my mom's surgery, and she started on her chemo treatments. It was like she had no time to recover as her body was hit with one thing after another. Seeing her so weak and sick all the time was a saddening feeling. I thought to myself that none of this was fair. My mother has always been a caring and kind woman who has done nothing but raise us with a self-sacrificing love. She didn't deserve this, and I became frustrated and felt so helpless. In my life I've been arrogant and selfish many times, and I wished I could take my mom's place and spare her from further pain.

My frustration turned to anger soon after. I wanted to hit somebody or smash something, but there was no one to blame. I've always wondered why bad things have to happen to good people, but I now believe that it is through such trials that we grow the most. It took me a few years to realize that my mom's suffering was meant to serve a far greater purpose for good. Through this, I've seen God use her to reach out and be an inspiration to cancer patients along with many others, and I've seen her faith strengthen firsthand. My mom has survived a horrible condition not by the skill of doctors alone or merely by chance, but instead, by her incredible willpower to see it to the end and by the grace of God, who will always guide and protect those who love Him.

Appendix D: Uriah's Story

How this felt to me, there's no simple way to explain—what I went through, what we all went through. I guess it's like receiving that perfect gift you've always wanted only to see it smashed before your eyes. Parents are like the Statue of Liberty, or the Twin Towers of New York: They're great monuments that inspire you to become more than you are and help give you passion and drive to live up to your own expectations and not someone else's. When we first heard of Mom not doing so well, I obviously was worried, but thought nothing of it. I thought it was just some ordinary problem that could be fixed with a dietary supplement or something like that. I was at a loss for words as it started getting worse and she was feeling sick all the time. I was worried she was really in pain.

I didn't know what to think as she had more and more doctors' appointments. As a kid I loved going to the doctor because it was cool then. It was heart-crushing when we received the diagnosis right before Christmas. At first I was fearful I might lose my mother, and she could be in a real bad medical condition the rest of her life. I prayed every night almost all night long. I was going to work every day but couldn't focus. I don't think I slept at all, from the time she was diagnosed until after surgery. I was worried and wondered if this was hereditary, how bad it was, what would happen in surgery, and how this could have been prevented or detected earlier!

Amidst all the anger, frustration, and worry, I found hope, as an overwhelming peace came over me. I knew the peace came from God as I stopped worrying and thanked Him for the victory He was going to give us. It was amazing because I knew there was going to be a miracle as they gave her only two years with chemotherapy. My family is still intact, and I know that no matter what happens, my mother will be healed in one form or another. The testimony of her story that I've lived through with her will encourage me the rest of my life. I know that perfect gift because I've had it all my life and it took the sunshine for me to finally see it!

Notes

I was born in the Holy Cross Hospital in Taos, New Mexico. Unknown to me, I was born with a deleterious mutation 187 del AG, which put me at high risk of developing some form of cancer by age seventy. The mutation was traced back to my mother's side. However, on my father's side, my paternal grandmother died of ovarian cancer in 1969. I had several paternal aunts who developed breast cancer in their forties, one who passed away just three months before my diagnosis. Paternal uncles were also diagnosed with colon cancer by age fifty. I never thought I'd be the next victim by age forty-five. I had a full-time job and life was busy; I didn't have time to slow down so I ignored the symptoms. When the diagnosis came, everything came to a screeching halt. My life would be forever changed.

References

Hordes, Stanley M. *To the End of the Earth.* New York, NY: Columbia University Press, 2005. This is the history of the Crypto Jews of New Mexico, the journey of Christopher Columbus, and the "Holy" Inquisition.

Golden, Gloria. *Remnants of Crypto-Jews Among Hispanic Americans.* Mountain View, CA: Floricanto Press, 2004.

Alexy, Trudi. *The Marrano Legacy: A Contemporary Crypto-Jewish Priest Reveals Secrets of His Hidden Life.* Albuquerque: The University of New Mexico Press, 2003.

Sanchez, Dell. *The Last Exodus.* Jubilee Alive Publications, 1998. A lot of history and explanation of name changes. A history of how the Sephardic Jews got to Spain in the first place.

Sanchez, Dell F., Ph. D. *Aliyah!: The Exodus Continues.* i Universe, Incorporated, 2001.

Alexy, Trudi. *The Mezuzah in the Madonna's Foot: Marranos and Other Secret Jews.* New York, NY: Simon & Schuster, 1993. This is the author's life history. She, too, discovered that she had Jewish roots and went back to Europe and interviewed people and wrote about the journey of families over the Pyrenees Mountains into Spain: "the rescued, the rescuers, etc. A lot of sad stories and success stories, again the hardships that people endured to save their lives."

When masses of Jews were converted to Catholicism, the names of these families were logged, of course, and thereafter the Catholic realm monitored them very closely. By the same token, we are able to do genealogy today because the Catholic church kept very good records of births, baptisms, marriages, etc. Again these are records of all the "Spanish" ancestors who fled from Spain to Mexico (or other countries), and then ended up moving farther north to Santa Fe, Santa Cruz, Picuris, etc.

Tobias, Henry. *A History of the Jews in New Mexico.* Albuquerque: University of New Mexico Press, 1990.

Herz, Cary. *New Mexico's Crypto-Jews.* Albuquerque: University of New Mexico Press, 2007. Named the best nonfiction book on religion by the National Federation of Press of Women. Photographs by: Cary Herz.

Colonial New Mexican Hispanic families with the BRCA1 187delAG Mutation

Paul R. Duncan, MD FACP

March 2010

Patricia's family has lived for generations in northern New Mexico. Her maternal aunt Maria has been the family historian and when I had the opportunity to discuss their family with Maria in 2007 she told me that she had traced the family back to members that were believed to be "Crypto Jews." She was aware of the research that we had carried out in Albuquerque in 2005 which identified an apparent increased frequency of familial breast and ovarian cancer in New Mexico women who identified themselves as having descended from the original colonial Hispanic settlers who came from Mexico beginning in the late 16th century and continuing through the early 18th century.

Patricia was the first member of her family to be found to have the BRCA1 187delAG mutation. In her book she describes the time of her diagnosis and that a number of years later the BRCA testing was ordered. In 2003 a group of researchers from the University of Colorado identified six unrelated non-Jewish Hispanic families from the San Luis Valley of Southern Colorado who all had apparent hereditary breast and ovarian cancer (HBOC). Within these families were members with cancer who were found to be carriers of the BRCA1 187delAG mutation (Mullineaux et al, Cancer 2003;98:597-602).

In 2005 I reported to the American Society of Clinical Oncology's annual meeting in Orlando, Florida that we had identified seven New Mexican Hispanic families with HBOC and five families identified themselves as having descended from Colonial Hispanic Settlers (Duncan, Proc Am Soc Clin Oncol 23:858s, 2005). All five of these families were found to carry the BRCA1 187delAG mutation. All of the families lived in Albuquerque and points north. I subsequently have had an opportunity to review with the University of Colorado investigators where the San Luis Valley families came from in New Mexico and they indicated that they had identified some who had originally settled in the Mora area and then moved into the San Luis Valley in the mid to late 19th c. We subsequently have updated our experience in a manuscript accepted for publication in 2010. We have identified in our clinic population 14 Hispanic families with a BRCA mutation and in 11 families who identified themselves as being descended from Colonial Hispanic Families all carried the same BRCA1 mutation-187delAG.

Dr. Stanley Hordes published in 2005 a book titled: *To the End of the Earth—A history of the Crypto-Jews of New Mexico* (Columbia University Press – New York). He makes a very compelling historical argument that a very real number of Spanish and Portuguese immigrants to the New World in the late 15th and 16th centuries were Jews (Sephardic) that left Spain because of the policies of the Holy Office of the Inquisition established in 1480. He has traced a number of families from Spain to Mexico and New Mexico beginning in 1598. He presents good evidence that supports that some of these families had been Jews in Spain and when immigrating to Mexico ultimately renounced their Jewish beliefs and converted to Catholicism (conversos) and some of the families continued to practice Judaism underground (crypto-Jews).

From my standpoint the important historical fact is that Spanish and Portuguese Jews left the Iberian Peninsula and carried with them the BRCA1 187delAG mutation that had originated in the Middle East. Jews migrating to the Iberian Peninsula carried this mutation as did Jews migrating in to central and eastern Europe. The other two mutations associated with Ashkenazi Jews developed at a later time. In New Mexico because of the remoteness of the area, these mutations tended to be concentrated within the Hispanic populations that settled here, and we see that effect today. At this point in time we do not know the frequency of this specific BRCA1 mutation in the Hispanic population of New Mexico, but we know from population studies of Hispanic populations that the BRCA1 187delAG mutation is the most common mutation identified in women with breast and/or ovarian cancer in Hispanic women.

It is important to identify in women with breast and ovarian cancer or ovarian cancer alone whether a BRCA mutation exists. When the mutation exists in a family, one expects 50% of family members to be carriers, and we have developed strategies to reduce a women's risk for getting breast and ovarian cancer. It is possible to be vigilant in families who have inherited these genes and to eliminate the devastating effects of cancer. It is important to recognize that the men in these families can carry the mutation and can pass it on to their sons and daughters. Men do get breast cancer and other cancers but at a much lower frequency that the women. It is important to note that in 2008 the US Congress passed a law named the Genetic Information Non-discrimination Act (GINA). This protects persons from health insurance discrimination because of genetic testing.

In Patricia's family, a goal of Patricia and many in her family is to encourage all individuals to undergo gene testing. If a mutation is found then cancer risk reduction strategies are available. Through this constant work, it is possible to significantly reduce the numbers of cancers diagnosed within the family; and if cancer is diagnosed, it can be found at an earlier potentially curable stage.

New Mexico Moms!
Stop Ovarian Cancer Being
The "Silent Killer"

Please read this information and pass it on to your friends and family:

Do you think that ovarian cancer only strikes post menopausal, childless women?

Do you feel protected because you have previously taken the Pill?

Do you think that there is no link between breast cancer and ovarian cancer?

Do you think that ovarian cancer is only caused by hormonal factors and not environmental ones?

If you answered "Yes" to any of the questions above, I strongly urge you to read on.

Hi, my name is Kay and I'm Mom to 5-year-old twins Abby and Hannah. Probably like you, three years ago, I thought ovarian cancer only struck post-menopausal women, and particularly those who had not had children. That lack of knowledge, and also ignoring what my body was very subtly trying to tell me, caused me to go from a clean gynecological bill of health in March of '06 to advanced stage ovarian cancer in November of that year. Now, nearly three years later, after an eight hour operation, six months of chemotherapy and two clinical drug trials, I am in remission. But as you will see, the story doesn't end here. That's why every women needs to know the warning signs and how to take action.

Ovarian Cancer is a cancer that forms in tissues of the ovary or in the surrounding peritoneal cavity (the inside wall surrounding the abdomen and uterus). There are two main types, the most common of which is ovarian epithelial carcinoma. This begins in cells on the surface of the ovary/peritoneal wall and accounts for 60-90% of all cases (www.ovariancancer.org). The spread of these cancerous cells induces fluid to build up, which quickly carries the malignant cells around the peritoneal cavity to organs as distant as the liver, lymph nodes, and diaphragm.

The Frightening Statistics (www.ovariancancer.org; www.seer.cancer.gov)

Most cancer statistics are frightening! but for ovarian cancer they are doubly so:

• Ovarian cancer occurs in 1 out of 72 women.

• The mean 5 year survival rate is 46%. For women under 65, it rises to 57%. Remember, though, that this includes women who have a recurrence and does not take account of staging. For advanced stage cancers, the rates are lower.

• About 15,000 women in the United States die from ovarian cancer each year.

• But most remarkably, If caught early, before the cancer has spread outside of the ovaries, the 5 year survival rate is 93%.

• Only 19% of cases are found this early (*NY Times* June 13, 2007 "Symptoms Found for Early Check on Ovary Cancer").

• First line treatment – hysterectomy (removal of uterus and ovaries), removal of tumors, chemotherapy – will allow 60-80% of advanced stage cancer patients to achieve full remission. Past research has done a very good job of removing almost all evidence of cancer through this approach. However, by its nature, microscopic epithelial cells tend to remain behind and can, after lying dormant for months or years, start to become active again. This is called recurrence.

• Around 80% of all women who reach full remission, through first line therapy, will have a recurrence.

As reported by Deborah Armstrong M.D, Johns Hopkins University (http://ovariancancer.jhmi.edu/recurrentqa.cfm):

• "We're good at getting people into the initial remission. We're just not so good at keeping them there."

• Although most cases of ovarian cancer are reported in women over 50 (the mean age at diagnosis is 63), 32% of cases are in women under 54 (www.ovariancancer.org). For women younger women than 45 its 13%.

• So what are the risk factors and symptoms and what can be done to avoid the trauma that this disease can bring to a family.

Risk Factors for Younger Women

(taken from www.wcn.org Women's Cancer Network)

• A mother or sister who has had breast cancer. The hereditary BRCA-1/2 genes carry mutations for both breast and ovarian cancer. If you have a family history of either, a blood test can evaluate your risk.

• You have endometriosis.

• You have low estrogen or have taken estrogen replacement therapy.

• You started menstruating early (before 12) or late (after 15).

• You have used fertility drugs.

• You have had long term exposure to unidentified environmental contaminants.

Symptoms

Cancer experts have identified a set of health problems that may be symptoms of ovarian cancer (*NY Times* June 13, 2007 "Symptoms Found for Early Check on Ovary Cancer"). This new advice is the first official recognition that ovarian cancer, long believed to give no warning until far advanced, causes symptoms at an earlier stage in many women.

The symptoms to watch out for are:

- bloating,
- pelvic or abdominal pain,
- difficulty eating, feeling full quickly,
- a change in bowel movements,
- a frequent or urgent need to urinate.

If you have any of these problems, nearly every day for more than two or three weeks, see a gynecologist, especially if the symptoms are new and quite different from your usual state of health.

On a personal note, I had at least three of these symptoms in the six months prior to my diagnosis, but who would think that bloating and gas was ovarian cancer! Now you need to at least consider that possibility.

Even if you don't have the symptoms, but can answer "yes" to at least two of the risk factors, ask your PCP for a CA-125 test at your annual physical (covered by most insurance). CA-125 is a protein produced by most ovarian tumor cells. Anything under 30 is considered normal but there are false positives, so don't panic if yours is elevated. It should just be re-checked in a few months, similar to smear test uncertainties, or followed up by an ultrasound.

In March '06, my CA-125 was 17. I asked for the test because I had been suffering from low estrogen since the birth of my twins and knew it was a risk factor. I also knew that bloating etc. were possible signs but felt "safe" because of the March test results. When a bladder infection, that wasn't cleared by antibiotics, sent me to the doctor in November, I was diagnosed with advanced stage ovarian cancer. My CA-125 was 4600! Even a few months can make a huge difference.

So I urge you to be aware and SHOUT OUT THIS MESSAGE to every women you know.

MAKE OVARIAN CANCER A KNOWN THREAT NOT A SILENT KILLER!

This information has been validated by Dr. Carolyn Muller of UNMH and the Cancer Institute of NM. It has been specifically prepared for pre-menopausal moms. More detailed information for older women can be found on any of the websites mentioned. You are welcome to contact me at Kay@OvarianCancerTogether.org or Tel. (505) 603 7878.

About the Author

Patricia Santistevan was born and raised as the second oldest of eight children in Taos, New Mexico. At age 46 she was diagnosed with ovarian cancer. Over the past 6 1/2 years she's gone through 5 re-currences, 2 major surgeries, and a total of 39 chemos. She now lives in Santa Fe, New Mexico, and has three sons.

You may contact the author at starpoetry@aol.com

Patricia at two years old

Patricia's Great Grandmother

Patricia on her trike

Krypto the Super Dog

Patricia and Aunt Amanda

Family photo the Christmas before my brother Joe passed away

Family photo after my brother Joe passed away

After first chemo session in 2004

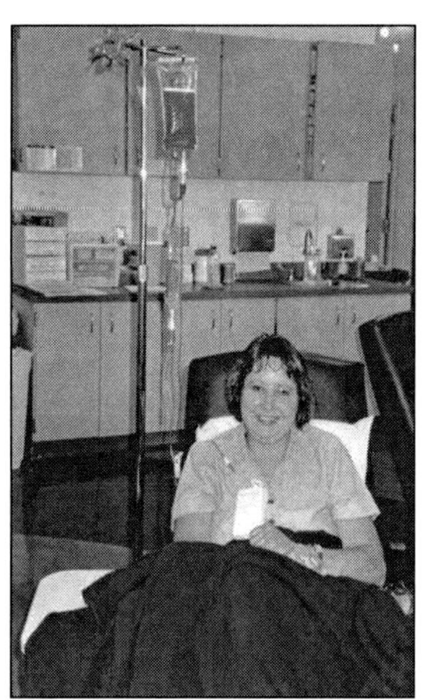

In chemo suite

My cancer support group

My sister and I volunteering at the Cancer Retreat

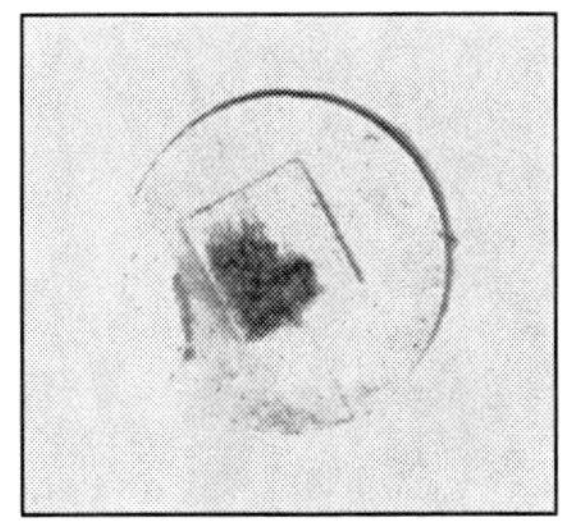

Heart shape on bandaid

First Glorieta Cancer Retreat

My mother and I at Glorieta Cancer Retreat

My Aunt Susie and I at her chemo treatment

My walk across the Golden Gate Bridge

My son on his wedding day

Let the healing rivers flow!

LaVergne, TN USA
07 September 2010
196092LV00002B/1/P